GARDENS
OF THE SOUL

CULTIVATING A

DEVOTIONAL LIFE

WITH GOD

DEBBONNAIRE
KOVACS

Pacific Press® Publishing Association
Nampa, Idaho
Oshawa, Ontario, Canada
www.pacificpress.com

Edited by B. Russell Holt
Designed by Michelle C. Petz
Cover illustration: © Linda Montgomery/SIS

Copyright © 2002 by

Pacific Press® Publishing Association
Printed in the United States of America
All Rights Reserved

Additional copies of this book may be purchased online at
www.adventistbookcenter.com

Unless otherwise indicated, all Bible quotations are from the New
American Standard Bible, 1973.

ISBN 0-8163-1872-7

02 03 04 05 06 • 5 4 3 2 1

Contents

This book is for my mother,
who first planted the seeds of God's love
in my soul's garden.

I would like to belatedly acknowledge
with deepest gratitude
the loving support and helpfulness
of Jerry D. Thomas, B. Russell Holt,
with special thanks to Aileen Sox, who first gave me
the nudge and encouragement I needed.

Aside from myself, the people named in the anecdotes of this book are fictional composite sketches or have had enough details changed to be beyond recognition. I pray you will recognize yourself and those you love in some of them and be blessed. And if you do, it is by the work of God, not because I meant to write about anyone in particular.

Introduction

"One is nearer God's heart in a garden than anywhere else on earth."[1] If you're a gardener, you know it's true. If you're not, you've heard gardeners quote these words—or similar ones—ad nauseam. My old copy of *Bartlett's Familiar Quotations* contains dozens of references to gardens and gardening, and the vast majority carry that same meaning. They point out that God planted the first garden and insist that people are happier and healthier in gardens than—well, than anywhere else on earth. I am wholly without prejudice or partiality in the matter. I am a gardener; therefore, I am one of those who know it's true!

It's probably because I am a gardener that one day I came up with the bright idea of reading the Bible as a "gardening manual." Among all the gardening and agricultural imagery there, surely I could find many delightful pictures of real, practical ways to cultivate my "inner garden," my devotional life with God. As I began, I was amazed at how rich a gold mine of information I had stumbled into. From choosing a garden site to planning, preparing, planting, and cultivating, all the way to harvest—it was all there—even droughts and winter seasons of waiting. I found practical insights into which part of the work is God's as the true Owner of the garden, which is mine as its caretaker, and how to do my work and cooperate with His. I found ways to deal with what we might call "pests and diseases," ways to increase harvests, and ways to wait out stormy weather. In plain English, I found allegories that help me, a visual person, to live my daily life closer to God, the greatest Master Gardener of all time.

Not unintentionally, this book will be very introspective, and thus self-focused. I believe that Christians, worried about being selfish, and rightly desiring to put others before themselves, are dangerously apt to dash into spiritual work for God and others to the neglect of their own devotional lives. We don't recognize that unless we tend the inner garden, there will be no fruit, and therefore no food to share with those who are needy.

On this point, here are quotations from two of my favorite authors:

The very essence of religion lies in the thought: Time with God. And yet how many of God's servants there are who, while giving their lives to His service, frankly confess that the feebleness of their spiritual life, and the inadequate results of their Christian service as a whole, are due to the failure to set aside time, and to use it rightly, for daily communion with God.[2]

I suggest there is a special, intimate place where we commune with the Father in a way that no one else can appreciate or understand. This place of the spirit I call the garden of our private world.[3]

Biblical writers . . . knew and taught that the development and maintenance of our inner worlds should be our highest priority. That is one practical reason that their work has transcended all times and cultures. For what they wrote they received from the Creator *who made us to work most effectively from the inner world toward the outer.*

One writer of Proverbs put the principle of the inner world in these words: "Watch over your heart with all diligence, for from it flow the springs of life," Proverbs 4:23.[4]

I discovered MacDonald's wonderful book after I was well into the writing of *Gardens of the Soul* and was so excited to find someone who thinks the way I do! He makes this invitation: "Frankly, I do not think we hear enough about these issues. And I would be delighted if some of these thoughts, which come from my heart and are borrowed from other thinkers and writers, begin a dialogue among a few curious people" p. 11.

I wholeheartedly agree! Let the dialogue begin.

---

[1] Dorothy Frances Blomfield Gurney, from the inscription at the Bok Singing Tower, Lake Wales, Florida.

[2] Parkhurst, Louis Gifford, Jr., ed., *The Believer's Secret of the Abiding Presence;* compiled from the writings of Andrew Murray and Brother Lawrence, Bethany House, 1978, p. 88.

[3] MacDonald, Gordon. *Ordering Your Private World.* Oliver Nelson, 1985, p. 10.

[4] Ibid., p. 23, emphasis supplied.

CHAPTER 1

God's Gardens: A Caretaker's Manual

It was God who planted the first garden—and planted His first children in it. It's interesting the way Genesis 2:8, 9 describes what God did. It doesn't say, "And God said, 'Let there be a garden.' " It says, "And the Lord God *planted* a garden toward the east, in Eden; and there He placed the man whom He had formed" (emphasis supplied). I don't know whether God knelt in the dirt to make Adam's and Eve's home, as He did to make them. But it almost sounds that way, doesn't it?

Later, when He had to send His beloved children away from the tree of life, God couldn't quit gardening. (No one can!) He's been gardening ever since—in human hearts. If ever a gardener had stony, weedy soil to contend with, He does! But like all gardeners, God is a dreamer.

You see, gardeners are a special breed of people. They see things no one else can see and do things no one else would do. And call it fun! Think of the most avid gardener you know. Who else could stand in the middle of a patch of thistles and quack grass with graph paper and pencils in his hands and stars in his eyes? Who else would stand ankle deep in a sand dune and say, "I think I'll have the pond over there!"? Who else would happily handle manure, pull weeds in July, with sweat running down her face in rivers, wrestle tillers and hoes, or get all excited when she opens her brightly wrapped birthday present and finds a thingamajig with a handle on one end and a scary looking spiked gizmo on the other?

Is God like that?

Look! There He is in the patch of thistles, and what is He saying? " 'Instead of the thorn bush the cypress will come up; and instead of the nettle the myrtle will come up; and it will be a memorial to the Lord, for an everlasting sign which will not be cut off' " (Isaiah 55:13).

See Him on the sand dune: "For waters will break forth in the wilderness and streams in the Arabah [desert]. And the scorched land will become a pool, and the thirsty ground springs of water" (Isaiah 35:6, 7).

What about the manure, the weeds, the backbreaking labor? Look at Luke 13:6-9. "And He [Jesus] began telling this parable: 'A certain man had a fig tree which had been planted in his vineyard; and he came looking for fruit on it, and did not find any. And he said to the vineyard-keeper, "Behold, for three years I have come looking for fruit on this fig tree without finding any. Cut it down! Why does it even use up the ground?" And he answered and said to him, "Let it alone, sir, for this year too, until I dig around it and put in fertilizer; and if it bears fruit next year, fine; but if not, cut it down." ' " Now, you know Jesus was not speaking of fig trees. He was talking about His kingdom. God has a lot invested in each of His children, just as the gardener had in this tree. He is not willing to give up on even one, no matter how much manure He has to use or how much digging He has to do.

Another thing God has in common with gardeners is the way He plans. Gardeners have a master landscaping plan, which covers all the land they own or can find an excuse to dig around in. For God, that's the whole world. He talks of sending " 'workers into His harvest' " (Matthew 9:38) where the " 'fields ... are white' " (John 4:35), and of "wheat and tares" growing together until the end (see Matthew 13:24-30) when He will " 'put in [His] sickle and reap' " (see Revelation 14:14-20).

The gardener's master plan is divided into distinct areas such as lawn, vegetable garden, ornamental garden, and orchard. God's plan has distinct areas too. He particularly speaks first of Israel, and then of the church as His garden or vineyard (see Isaiah 5:1-7). Especially notice verse 7: "The vineyard of the Lord of hosts is the house of Israel, and the men of Judah His delightful plant." Then see Jesus' exposition of this parable in Matthew 21:33-44 and recognize the promise inherent in verse 43: " 'Therefore I say to you, the kingdom of God will be taken away from you, and be given to a nation producing the fruit of it.' "

Finally, in each gardener's personal kingdom, there are little spots he calls "gardens," which may be no bigger than a few square feet, but which are very special in his eyes. From the "mailbox garden," to the "shade garden" under the big maple, to the "fragrance garden" around his favorite lawn chair—these mini-gardens are the heart of the whole plan. Without them, there would be no garden.

In this book, we're going to concentrate on God's mini-gardens in your heart and mine. The gardens of our souls belong to God; He makes the plans and decisions and does all the real work. But He invites us to be His caretakers or stewards. We can work out what God works in, toiling side by side with Him to cultivate and develop the life of our own souls. It's exciting, awesome, and sometimes pretty scary work! It's easy, too, to try to take over God's work—or fail to do ours. Think of this book as a "caretaker's manual." We'll examine the work God and we—His caretakers—do together, sharing tips, tools, and insights and pointing out possible pitfalls. The first chapters will deal mostly with God's work in us and our cooperation with that work. Then, in later chapters, we will learn more about our part of the work and how to help (or at least not hinder!) the growth of the virtues and blessings God plants in our hearts. We'll also realize more fully that He never stops working and that our work, at its shining best, is useless or even destructive without Him. Most of all, we'll see how our Master Gardener treasures each one of His mini-gardens—no matter what they may look like to us.

Let me share with you a passage you probably don't know is in the Bible. It goes like this: "Indeed, the Lord will comfort Debbonnaire; He will comfort all her waste places; and her wilderness He will make like Eden, and her desert like the garden of the Lord; joy and gladness will be found in her, thanksgiving and sound of a melody" (see Isaiah 51:3). You never read that before, did you? Believe me, every word of it is true.

The Master Gardener has another special garden too. Listen: " 'The Lord will continually guide you [*you!*], and satisfy your desire in scorched places, and give strength to your bones; and you will be like a watered garden, and like a spring of water whose waters do not fail' " (Isaiah 58:11).

In the secret places of your heart, deep inside where no one else can ever enter—not even the closest people you love the most—there is a locked garden. According to Song of Solomon 4:12-15, it is a rock garden with a spring at its heart. Within its silent walls a rich variety of tropical delights may thrive, from pomegranates and choice fruits to cinnamon, frankincense, myrrh, and all the finest spices. Jesus says to you, " 'You are a garden spring, a well of fresh water, and streams flowing from Lebanon' " (verse 15). He knocks at your locked gate and calls, " ' "Open to me ... my darling" ' " (5:2)! And He longs for you to answer, " 'May my beloved come into his garden and eat its choice fruits!' " (4:16).

But you know what really grows in that garden. You are the one who has to live there. What if there are no choice fruits? What if your garden feels more like a blackened ruin? What if sand and thistles are your biggest crops?

Angela first heard the concept of using garden imagery to represent the inner self from her psychiatrist. On the outside, she was the woman who had everything. She was married to a wealthy, upcoming businessman, drove the most expensive cars, wore the costliest clothes, and sent her children to top-notch private schools. Yet Angela, for no reason that she could understand, grew more and more miserable. She found herself drinking more, snapping at her husband, and slapping her children. In desperation, she went to a psychiatrist who was well-known among her friends as being a spiritual leader. When he asked her to think of her heart as a garden and tell him what she saw there, Angela began to cry.

"It's just a ruin," she sobbed. "Nothing is there—nothing alive!"

The psychiatrist promised he could help her. He told her she needed a more spiritual life, and over the next few weeks recommended such things as hypnosis, channeling, and meditation with the help of what he called a spirit guide. Angela tried everything he suggested.

At first it seemed to work. Angela had a new focus, a new interest in her life. Then one day, as she was telling a friend of her experiences, the friend asked, "So what grows in the garden now?"

Angela stared at her friend a moment. And then the tears began again. "There's still nothing. Sometimes I think about killing myself."

Did you notice, in the stories of Isaiah 5 and Matthew 21, what happens to God's garden when it has any other keepers but the Owner, who loves it? The picture is even more graphic in Jeremiah 12:10, 11. " 'Many shepherds [shepherds, no less!] have ruined My vineyard, they have trampled down My field; they have made My pleasant field a desolate wilderness. It has been made a desolation, desolate, it mourns before Me.' " Have you ever felt that way? Do you mourn before Him? Are you afraid to let Him in? If so, it may be that, like Angela, you have been allowing other gardeners, with their brilliantly colored, deceptive seed catalogs and promises of great harvests, to wreak havoc in your secret garden.

Or maybe you have been trying to keep up with all the weeding, tilling, and what-have-you on your own. Pete was a deeply spiritual Christian. He yearned to be the man God wanted him to be. One night in his bedroom, he made a list of all the worst sins he could think of in his life. Then he asked God for help and went to work to eliminate them. Bad temper was first on the list. Whenever Pete was tempted to shout at someone, he bit his tongue and counted to ten. Or to fifty. If he thought of it, he would say a Bible verse as well. Soon, Pete could go for a whole week without losing his temper—out loud, anyway. He crossed temper off his list and went to work on laziness.

He set his alarm for one hour earlier in the morning. This gave him time to read his daily devotional book and exercise before getting ready for work. In the evenings, he got busy on all the jobs around the house that he had been putting off. After two weeks of this regimen, his wife said plaintively that she appreciated his hard work, but she wished he had more time to spend with her. Pete blew his stack. He actually called his wife a name! He was shocked and dismayed, and immediately apologized. But that night Pete heard his wife, whom he loved deeply, stifling tears. Getting out of bed, he drew a red circle around "temper" on his list and added, "Be more loving to Linda." He stayed up for hours, pacing, berating himself, and pleading with God to forgive him.

The next morning Pete overslept and was late to work.

Pete was ready to give up. He felt as if the harder he tried, the more out of control everything was. And all he wanted was to do the right thing. Where, he wondered angrily, was God?

Pete didn't know that the Master Gardener had counsel for him. In Isaiah 17:10, 11, God warns, "You have forgotten the God of your salvation and have not remembered the rock of your refuge. Therefore you plant delightful plants and set them with vine slips of a strange god. In the day that you plant it you carefully fence it in, and in the morning you bring your seed to blossom; but the harvest will be a heap in a day of sickliness and incurable pain."

Have you, like Pete, been working desperately to make your garden a place where Jesus will love to visit? Are you shocked to discover that in God's eyes your carefully tended righteousness is "vine slips of a strange god"? After all, the plants you have planted are delightful ones, and certainly ones God wants in your garden. But doing the work yourself is Satan's favorite false doctrine for Christians. If you and Pete do not want to end with your life in a shambles, you *must* learn to let God do His own gardening.

Perhaps, unlike these people, you have just been letting things go wild, trusting them to grow the way they should. James is like that. He thinks he's a pretty good guy. He has his faults, but doesn't everybody? All this heart searching, in his opinion, is just a waste of time. Live and let live, that's his motto. He doesn't even look around his garden much. If he did, he'd find that instead of the wildflower meadow he imagines, he has a barren desert or a rank jungle it would take a machete to hack through.

The problem is, as we learned in the parable of the fig tree, God expects His trees to bear fruit. If you "just stand there," so to speak, refusing to let God in to do His work, or ignoring what He tries to do, you are in very scary territory. At least Angela and Pete realize they need help. They are in a good position to hear and recognize God's voice when He says to them—through a friend, a pastor, a song—"I'm still knocking. Please let Me in. I've got My hoe with Me." James, believing he is in need of nothing, is not even listening, and God may have to resort to more drastic measures to get his attention.

And if James refuses to listen? Well, Jesus added a frightening postscript to that fig tree parable during the last week of His earthly life. He was on His way back to Jerusalem the day after the triumphal entry. He was feeling hungry that morning and was happy to see a fig tree. Fig trees produce their fruit before their leaves, so this one looked very promising—the image of a beautiful, healthy fig tree. But Jesus looked in vain for fruit. The tree looked great on the outside, but its promise was empty. Seeing an opportunity to impress a spiritual lesson on the disciples He would leave so soon, Jesus said, " 'No longer shall there ever be any fruit from you.' And at once the fig tree withered" (Matthew 21:19).

But don't worry. Have you been noticing a lot of upheaval and—well, not to put too fine a name to it—manure in your life lately? That's God, digging and fertilizing. Please don't ignore Him!

January. Everything is cold, still, silent. Nothing seems to be alive. It's hard to believe anything will ever live again. But look through the warm, lighted windows of God's potting shed. There He is, doing the same thing every other gardener is doing this time of year. He's poring over His seed catalogs and graph paper, eyes alight with anticipation. He's dreaming about you. Listen! Hear Him whispering? "And _____ will be like a tree firmly planted by streams of water, which yields its fruit in its season, and its leaf does not wither; and in whatever s/he does, s/he prospers" (see Psalm 1:3).

DIG DEEPER

Have you ever thought of your inner self as a garden? If not, while reading this book you may wish to experiment with the idea. Close your eyes and prayerfully imagine what your garden might be like. What are some of the secret things you share with God and no one else? Ask God to show you what He would like to see growing in your garden. Try to determine if things are growing there that you thought were good, but which are your ideas, not the Master Gardener's. This will take time—your whole life, in fact. The earlier you begin, the better.

Look up some of the texts used in this chapter and read them in context. Prayerfully determine which most apply to you. Do you feel as if your garden is a jungle you can't even find your way through? Does God need to do some clearing and ordering? Or do you feel like a dry, arid sand dune? Do you need the spring of the Holy Spirit? Is your garden growing well, as you seek to live each day in the Gardener's hand? Ask Him to show you new delights, new places He'd like to dig up to enlarge your borders and your ability to be a blessing to others.

Can you see yourself as more like Angela, who to her regret, let others plant her garden—and not God? Are you like Pete, who tried to do his own gardening? Or James, who believes in the live-and-let-live school of gardening? Or is there a different way you could characterize your gardening style?

It would be a great idea to begin a gardening journal, writing to God about the things that you learn as you study the concept of soul gardening with Him. You might begin by writing a description of your garden as you see it now, your gardening style, and a prayer committing yourself to working with God in whatever ways He wants to show you.

Snapshots From My Garden

Through an arid waste, the Gardener strode, backpack creaking, tool belt jangling. His eyes never stopped moving, left to right, right to left, searching . . . searching. At last, around a granite outcropping, over a cliff, deep in a silent, shadowed corner of the silent, shadowed land, He stopped. A smile creased His dusty face. There! Under the overhang, behind the rubble, almost invisible, but not quite . . .

He moved slowly, watchfully. No sign of life, no eye peeking from the . . . structure? The Gardener's smile twisted a little. It was more a pile of rubble, actually. A hodgepodge of boards, bricks, stones, and mud. Layer upon layer, carefully and thoroughly fastened together over years of soul-wrenching effort, with nails, glue, pins, staples, and concrete. It was pitifully camouflaged with dead branches.

The Gardener inched His way around the mess, but found no apparent means of entry or exit. Not too loudly, He knocked on a board. There was no answer, but the Gardener's keen ears heard the quickened heartbeat within.

Gently, He called a name. Still no answer, but the skitter of the heartbeat escalated painfully. "Come, little one. Please let Me in. You will be safe."

Silence. Then a frantic whisper. "How do You know my name?"

The Gardener saw a crack between two stones. If He peered in, would it frighten her further? More quietly still, He said, "I know you. And I would never hurt you. Please, may I come in?"

He waited.

At length an eye appeared at the crack. The Gardener stood still while the eye measured Him and counted His tools. "Why do You want to come in?"

"I'd like to buy your . . . fortress."

"Buy it! Why?"

"I like it."

The eye watched Him warily. The Gardener waited.

"How much?"

"Fifty billion dollars."

There was a gasp and a choking noise from within the structure. "You're joking!"

"No. Furthermore, you may continue to live here, and I will build you a new home—a walled garden."

"This is already a walled garden. I happen to have a lot of plants in here."

The Gardener controlled His smile. "I can build a better one. Let Me in, and we'll talk about it."

"I, I would . . . really. But you see . . . well, there's no door."

"I can make one." There was no answer, so the Gardener took His hammer from His tool belt and pried loose a board.

There was a shriek, and He stepped back. A white face appeared in the gap, squinting in the light and crying. "What are You doing?" A shaking hand scrabbled for the broken board.

The Gardener grabbed the hand, and the struggle began. It was a struggle between life and death, but only He knew it. He held on, murmuring soothingly, until the fighting and screaming subsided to trembling and sniffles. He waited, still talking quietly, until He felt another cold, damp hand join the first, clinging to His.

"Please," He whispered, "Let Me in."

And He waited.

CHAPTER 2

Choosing a Site: Gardening the Hard Way

In order to move beyond dreaming over seed catalogs to actually planting a garden, you have to choose a garden site. And as soon as we begin to look around at the sites God chooses for His gardens, it becomes apparent that our Master Gardener loves a challenge. Anyone can make a successful garden if the site has perfect soil, perfect terrain, and a perfect climate. But God likes to show what He can do with deserts, swamps, and jungles. Why is that?

Well, let's see the reason He gives in Isaiah 41:19, 20: " 'I will put the cedar in the wilderness, the acacia, and the myrtle, and the olive tree; I will place the juniper in the desert, together with the box tree and the cypress, *that they may see and recognize, and consider and gain insight as well, that the hand of the Lord has done this, and the Holy One of Israel has created it'* " (emphasis supplied). God wants to be visible; He wants to be recognized in our world. And this is one of the ways He chooses to make Himself known. He does the impossible so there will be no mistaken notion that it was done by human hands or minds.

But no one—not even the Master of the universe—can just go around gardening anywhere He pleases. First He has to find the property.

" 'The kingdom of heaven is like a treasure hidden in the field, which a man found and hid' " (Matthew 13:44). Usually we look at this parable as representing the treasure of the gospel that is worth everything we could possibly give up for it—and immeasurably more. But did you ever look at this parable backward? I recently heard a preacher say that maybe God thinks *I* am a treasure hidden in the dirt! Could it be true? Does God really wander the wildernesses and jungles of this world, searching for treasures He considers beyond price? Yes! I've seen Him do it, and so have you. Maybe you've seen His determination and persistence at work in your own life. Maybe things have happened to you that you know perfectly well, no matter what rationalizations you cook up, should never have happened. Maybe you ran and ran, and every time you turned around, there He was, still holding out His arms to you.

Once He finds the property He wants, He has to buy it. " 'From joy over it he goes and sells all that he has, and buys that field' " (verse 44). How much did Jesus sell to buy you—or even for the right to ask you if He could plant a garden in your life? Believe it or not, you and I still have to give our permission to the proposed project.

So He comes to you. He knocks politely. " ' "Behold, I stand at the door and knock" ' " (Revelation 3:20). " ' "Open to me ... my darling" ' " (Song of Solomon 5:2)!

If you say No, He won't go away. He'll keep trying, especially if one of His other children is praying for you. But He'll never force your door open even though He's already paid full price for your property.

There are a lot of ways of barricading oneself away from God. The most obvious is the person who simply refuses to have anything to do with God, Christ, or religion in any form. You may know people like that. You may even have been like that, but if you are reading this book, you have, at least, cracked the door. Let's look at some less obvious, but still deadly ways we lock ourselves away from the Master Gardener.

Marietta spends quite a lot of time thinking about her thoughts and feelings. She takes pride in the fact that she is very "internally aware," compared to some of her friends, who seem to just go about their lives with no idea what is going on inside them. She takes seriously Peter's admonition to be ready to give a reason for one's hope and faith (see 1 Peter 3:15), and when someone questions her, she is very articulate in her answers. Marietta knows her garden needs improvement, but she has the improvements well in hand. If she lets Jesus all the way in (she loves to talk to Him over the fence), He might . . . well, He might mess things up. He might require things of her that she does not feel prepared or qualified to do. He might even do things that would humiliate her, things that would make her look like a fool. In Marietta's considered opinion, nothing in life is worse than looking foolish. But lately, when she talks to the Master Gardener over the fence, He's been more insistent that she let Him all the way in. When she balks, He asks her to step outside with Him. If she gives in and goes out, He'll shock her by showing her the name on her handsome, well-designed barricade. It's "Selfishness." She's paying more attention to herself and her own needs— and what people might think of her or what God might do to her— than she is to Jesus and *His* plans for her garden.

Ana, on the other hand, doesn't think her garden needs anything at all. That is, she would think the idea of a garden inside her ridiculous, but if she *does* have one, it's fine, thank you. She has gone to church for all of her seventy years, pays tithe faithfully, prays and reads a devotional book daily. If she hears any knocking, she assumes it's the world, the flesh, or the devil, because, of course, God is right inside with her, sitting in the chair next to hers, with His hands folded in His lap like hers. Ana is trapped behind an extremely dangerous, almost unbreakable barricade called "Complacency." If God is to get her out from behind it, He may have to take a bulldozer to it. He can do that, even without her permission, especially if someone is praying for her. The question is: If He risks it, will she let Him through the inner door that only she can open? Or will she blame Him and lock herself even deeper away?

Lee is—was—a deeply devoted Christian. When his parents died while he was still young, leaving him to fend for himself, it was as though a great tree in his garden had fallen, breaking part of his foundations.

But he pushed aside his bitterness and questions, knowing God would get him through. And He did. Lee was even able to find grants, loans, and jobs to take him through college. Then a war came, and he had to leave college and serve his country. Once again Lee buried his anger and tried to pick up the wreckage and go on. Overseas, Lee lost his leg. When he came home, he lost his girl too. Suddenly, and shockingly, all the anger, doubts, and bitterness he had buried through the years exploded, destroying what was left of his soul's garden.

Lee's had it. He's had it with God, with church, and with life in general. He's tired of trying. In utter fury, he has nailed up barriers of "Rage" all the way around his life, crawled inside, and battened down the hatches. But the Gardener is still knocking, still calling. His greatest hope is that maybe one of these days Lee will get tired of the continual hounding, open the door, and scream at *Him*—pour out all his frustration and pain and anger, ask all his questions, pound his fists on Jesus' broad chest, and finally fall into His arms and cry. Then, and only then, will Lee be able to begin to heal.

But probably the most common human response to God is fear. It's the only logical response. We have been so cut off and isolated from reality that anything outside the realm of what we see every day—what we think is reality—is terrifying. In the Bible, every time someone saw an angel, the first thing the angel had to say was, "Don't be afraid!" As a child, I saw an angel myself, and I screamed. That's been the response of most of those I've known or heard of who came in contact with God's reality. The problem is that even after God says, "Be not afraid! It is I!" a lot of us stay scared.

Sharon could tell you. First, she was afraid God didn't even exist. Then she was afraid that He couldn't really care for her—not if He really knew anything about her. Little by little, over the fence, so to speak, Sharon learned who God was and that He wanted only the best for her. But she was still afraid to really let Him in. What would He do? Worse yet, what would He make *her* do? Finally, she let Him in. Her life began that day, and she was so overcome that she couldn't believe she had ever been afraid. Imagine her dismay when, as the years passed, she still found herself frightened by every new thing He proposed even as she saw the joy and beauty the Gardener had created in her soul. Sometimes, just as if she'd never learned a thing, just as if she didn't love Him, just as if she didn't think He loved her, she still holed up in a corner, and He had to coax her out.

Then, maybe worst of all, there's "Guilt." This is one of the most impassable barriers, because it looks right! Just take a good look at yourself! If your garden were a wilderness only because it had never yet been tamed, that would be one thing. But who dug up and trashed that beautiful rose bed? Who tore down the wall in one corner and built it as high as possible, elsewhere—with glass and barbed wire on it? Who threw trash in the pond and turned it into a scummy, smelly, unsightly mess? Who let in the locusts and ignored the poison ivy until they took over the whole place? *You* did! You know it, and He knows it, and you know He knows it! How can you possibly have the colossal nerve to ask Him to come in and clean up the mess you made?

Sound familiar? It does to me! I've been there, done that, didn't like it! This very week, in church, I had to be reminded again. A dear friend showed me a text I had read a million times and never known was there. Here is what it says, along with my friend's commentary: "The sorrow that is according to the will of God [that's realizing you have sinned and being truly remorseful for it] produces a repentance without regret, leading to salvation; but the sorrow of the world [that's the guilt you keep carrying around with you even after you know you're forgiven] produces death" (2 Corinthians 7:10). To be perfectly honest, I found it hard to imagine a repentance without regret. My regrets seem to hang on for years and years. But if I *could* find that kind of peace, if I could really let go of those regrets, I knew that getting rid of that guilt would produce salvation as the verse says. Besides, I recognized the voice clearly, even though it was cloaked in my friend's voice. My beloved Master Gardener was speaking to me through her. At home, He and I talked it out. I said, "Yes, take it away." Now, when thoughts of guilt for past, forgiven offenses fly into my garden like pesky Japanese beetles, I'll aim a good strong spray of 2 Corinthians 7:10 at them. And to prevent myself from building a new barrier, whether of guilt, fear, or anything else, I'll ask the Gardener to give me a job to keep me busy. Maybe I can help break new ground. There's nothing like swinging a heavy mattock for making it easy to sleep at night!

Say Yes! Then the adventure begins. A sign goes up in front of the mess at your garden site. In big, colorful letters, it says:

FUTURE HOME OF

A NEW GARDEN OF EDEN.

LANDSCAPE DESIGN BY YAHWEH.

At first it's hard to believe. Nothing is there but heaps of dirt and piles of lumber and rubbish. But the sound of earth-moving equipment and the smell of excitement are in the air!

DIG DEEPER

Have you allowed God to choose you for a new garden site? If not, why not decide right now to let Him in, all the way in, once and for all?

What kind of barriers have you built against the true indwelling power of God through His Spirit? Are there any barriers up now in your life? If so, what will you do about them?

Write in your journal about the differences that have taken place in your inner garden since Jesus came in.

Snapshots From My Garden

He was in. And it was her own fault. She remembered saying Yes. She shivered in a corner and watched Him gaze around her fortress as if He were memorizing everything He saw. Blinding, dusty light slanted through the opening He had broken in her wall. It made things look different, and her eyes followed His around the space. There were her carefully tended plants in little pots along the wall, looking strangely yellow and spindly. The sound of scurrying in corners and buzzes above her head showed that there were others here, no matter how carefully sealed she kept the walls. They were disturbed by the light as she was. She would have to mend that hole He had made.

The Gardener had stopped in the center of the room, looking at the Tree. The Tree was the center of her life—the center of everything. As she blinked in the light, sudden tears welled in her eyes. The Tree looked weak and sad—almost stunted. When she thought of all she had done to try to protect it . . . She squealed in fear as the Man took a sharp tool from His belt and knelt to dig in the dirt below the Tree. He stopped immediately and turned toward her. When she saw His eyes, she felt strange. They made her think of the way His hand had held her. Strong. Safe.

Putting down the tool, He held both hands out this time. She watched them for a minute, then slid toward them. Held against His heart, she forgot everything else and didn't think—just felt.

She got His shoulder soggy.

Finally, she sniffled, rubbed her nose on the sleeve that wasn't torn, and pulled back to look around again at her castle. "It's . . . ugly!" she whispered. "Why? I've tried so hard."

"It's all right now. You'll see. The first thing we need is water. See here where the ground is muddy?" He pointed to where He had started to dig.

She nodded hesitantly. "I tried to keep it dry."

He smiled. "I know. But you're thirsty, and so is your tree and all your plants. I will make a spring here. Would you like to help Me?"

She wasn't sure.

"Watch," He said. He took up His tool again, and she flinched. But she

watched. And as He dug, water began to seep, then to bubble, right out of the ground at the roots of her Tree. It was brown and thick, but it caught the light and sparkled just a little as it rolled toward the lowest corner of the room. It was getting away! She ran to try to catch it with her hands.

The Gardener called her back. "Don't be afraid, Beloved. There is plenty of water. Enough to last forever. Enough to share. Come." He held out another tool like His, but smaller. "We'll make a little pool right here to catch enough water for you and your plants."

Clumsily, she helped Him dig. After a while, they had a little round pool. When they stopped digging, the water began to settle and clear. Now the light danced on its surface and made her squint. "There!" He seemed delighted. "Have a drink."

Cautiously, she tasted some. It was strange. Cold. There was no dirt in it. She had never had water with no dirt in it. She wasn't sure if she liked it. But she found she couldn't stop drinking it until she was full. Next, they carried little jars of water to all the plants along the walls. The plants almost seemed to sigh in gratitude.

When they were through, the Gardener looked around with a satisfied air. She followed His gaze as she had before, but with a new feeling. She was glad she had let Him in, after all. It was much nicer. Now she would be able to tend her Tree and her plants, and everything would be fine, just as He had said.

"Now," said the Gardener, "for the walls."

"Oh, no," she said. "You don't have to mend it. I've decided it's OK to have a little light. It feels kind of warm."

The Gardener laughed and put His arm around her shoulders. "You don't understand. We need much more light than this. The walls will have to come down."

She screamed and twisted away from Him. "Come down?! NO!!" Why had she let Him in? He would destroy everything she had spent a lifetime building!

He held her again and waited until she could listen.

"See the water?" He pointed toward the low corner of the room. The spring had overflowed again and was puddling up and making a muddy mess in the corner. "It needs a way to get out. We'll build a little conduit *there. Then, after these walls are down, we will build a strong, beautiful, low wall with a watchtower for protection. I will always keep you safe. There is nothing to fear."*

It took some convincing. But when He quietly asked her, "Do you want Me to leave?" and she looked into His sad eyes, something broke open inside her.

"Do You want to go?"

"No!" He held her face in both hands. "Never!"

"Don't go," she whispered.

And she went and covered her head in a corner while He picked up His sledgehammer.

CHAPTER 3

Breaking Ground: God's Dynamite

Before you even sign the contract, your Master Gardener is bubbling over with plans and promises. " 'I chose you, and appointed you, that you should go and bear fruit, and that your fruit should remain, that whatever you ask of the Father in My name, He may give to you' " (John 15:16). "[You] will be like a tree firmly planted by streams of water, which yields its fruit in its season, and its leaf does not wither" (Psalm 1:3). " 'Your shoots are an orchard of pomegranates with choice fruits, henna with nard plants, nard and saffron, calamus and cinnamon, with all the trees of frankincense, myrrh and aloes, along with all the finest spices' " (Song of Solomon 4:13, 14).

How can that happen? How can there be such a tropical feast where once there was only desolation? " 'You are a garden spring, a well of fresh water, and streams flowing from Lebanon' " (verse 15).

First, nothing grows without water. And you're already in trouble, because either there is no water at all on your site or what is there is poisoned and mucky and green, right? That's OK; this Gardener brings His own water—a permanent supply. " 'Whoever drinks of the water that I shall give him shall never thirst; but the water that I shall give him shall *become in him a well* of water springing up to eternal life' " (John 4:14, emphasis supplied).

God says, " 'The afflicted and needy are seeking water, but there is none, and their tongue is parched with thirst; I, the Lord, will answer them Myself, as the God of Israel I will not forsake them. I will open rivers on the bare heights, and springs in the midst of the valleys; I will make the wilderness a pool of water, and the dry land fountains of water' " (Isaiah 41:17, 18). You see, *then* He can plant the cedar and acacia and myrtle and so forth. First, there's work to be done.

You will not be alone if you are rather dismayed at what happens after you say Yes to this divine Dreamer. First, it often looks as if nothing at all is happening. He spends a lot of time walking your property and peering into dark corners and asking you searching questions, all with a notepad in His hand. You point out assets you think are valuable, and He smiles and nods. You remind Him nervously that there is no water source for the gardens He plans and tell Him the disasters that have occurred the few (or many) times you've tried to plant anything. He gazes up at a particularly forbidding cliff in your landscape and says, "Don't worry. I'll take care of that." Then He steps aside and waves His arm, and you begin to tremble at the vibration of a fleet of huge, earth-moving equipment. Stunned, you open your mouth to protest and then remember that, after all, He bought the place, and presumably He knows what He's doing. You take a deep breath and determine to weather the assault. Then you see the guys with cases of dynamite.

Take a closer look at Isaiah 41:18. " 'I will *open* rivers on the bare heights, and springs in the midst of the valleys' " (emphasis supplied). What do you think that means, anyway? Even when He just points His finger and speaks the word as He did at Creation (and sometimes He chooses to do that), there is still an upheaval and landslide.

Let's face an unpalatable truth here. When Jesus comes to our door, like a salesman, with a briefcase full of bright promises, He doesn't tell us up front everything He plans to do to bring all these promises to fruition. If He did, we'd probably turn Him away every time. Turning a desert, swamp, jungle, or whatever into the garden of the Lord is heavy, dirty, time-consuming, sometimes heartbreaking work.

You have several choices here. First, you can send Him away. Even though He has already paid the full price and, by rights, you belong to Him, He works only on an open-ended contract. You can change your mind and remain a desert, swamp, or whatever. Lucifer was the first to irrevocably make this choice. Many more have made it since. I, for one, don't believe their Father will ever fully recover from their loss.

Second, you can argue, complain, and try to talk Him around to your way of thinking. This is not likely to work, but many have tried it anyway. The Israelites are a good example. And the truth is, so are we sometimes.

When Lamar's friends told him he shouldn't be spending so much time with a married woman, he laughed at them. "Don't be silly! We're just friends!" As time went on, though, the feelings began to change. Lamar knew he should stop seeing Linda.

When he mentioned it to her, she protested, "We're not doing anything wrong! My husband doesn't understand me! What would I do if I couldn't talk to you?" So they continued to meet. Lamar justified the situation by telling himself and God that he was trying to help Linda with her difficult marriage. He even prayed with her and tried to help her grow closer to God.

When Linda's marriage ended, Lamar tried to convince himself that he was sorry, that he had done all he could to try to save it. But secretly, he wondered if they were meant for each other after all, now that she was free. He began to pray seriously, "Lord, all I want is Your will. I know if You don't want us together, then we wouldn't be happy. I'll give Linda up if You want me to." Lamar really meant what he said. But a strange thing was happening in his devotional life. Whenever he prayed about this situation, he found himself despairing—even crying. Why? Why couldn't he hear God's answer? Years later, Lamar would tell a similarly situated young man, "Break it off *before* it's strong enough to hurt! I know now my tears should have shown me that deep in my heart, I already knew God's answer was No. Even though I really did want to please Him, I was trying desperately to convince Him that my way was better than His."

Notice the very next verse following the promises we've been reading in Isaiah. " 'Present your case,' the Lord says. 'Bring forward your strong arguments,' the King of Jacob says" (Isaiah 41:21). The rest of the chapter makes the point that work done by anyone else is "of no account" and "amounts to nothing" (verse 24.) Then, God says, " 'Behold, *My* Servant' " (Isaiah 42:1, emphasis supplied). "He is the One who will do the best job. Trust Me." Even with all that blasting going on and your life in apparent turmoil, " 'a bruised reed He will not break, and a dimly burning wick He will not extinguish' " (verse 3).

Whether they marry or not, God will never stop working with and for Lamar and Linda. But they may argue themselves into giving Him up entirely, refusing His love and help, and plugging their ears to block out His voice.

Third, you can grit your teeth, square your shoulders (or hide your head), and try to bear it—with or without arguing about it. Elijah tried this approach. His story is told in 1 Kings 19. Elijah had obediently done everything God told him to do. He had warned King Ahab, lived through the drought with the widow and her boy, gone through the whole Mount Carmel incident, and prayed the rain back again. He might have been excused for thinking he was a pretty good guy. But none of us ever get to the point that we no longer need any ground breaking done in our hearts. Elijah saw the fuse burning on the dynamite when he got this ominous message from Queen Jezebel: " 'So may the gods do to me and even more, if I do not make your life as the life of one of them by tomorrow about this time' " (verse 2).

So he ran and hid, hung his head, and prayed a memorable prayer: "I give up, God. Just let me die." Have you ever prayed that? I have.

God encouraged Elijah by feeding him miraculous angel food that gave him the strength to hike forty days and nights, but when he got to the mountain of God, he had recovered only marginally. He hid in a cave, told God he was the only faithful one left, and seemed prepared to just sit out the rest of his life there. Where else should one hide from trouble, after all?

An enormous number of Christians take Elijah as their role model in trial. They think this is what God expects. And I must admit that a number of times in my life I couldn't manage any more than this, either. I suppose it's better than arguing, and it's certainly better than canceling the contract altogether. But it's not as good as . . .

Forth, you can enter into His excitement. You can lean over His shoulder and try to make sense of His graph paper and notes. (You usually can't, but it's fun to try.) You can seek God's voice in the wind and fire and earthquake, and learn to quiet down and listen while His still, small voice whispers in your ear, "I was right here all along. You are not the only faithful one left, and I still have a job for you to do." You can ask Him to show you your share in His work, and willingly, if ineptly, wield the pick or shovel He gives you. (Don't, don't, *don't* do anything unless He tells you to!) You can even stand right beside Him, gripping His hand, while that cliff you thought was the foundation of your life blows sky high. Yes, you can, even with tears in your eyes. You just have to hang on for dear life.

Also, you can, and probably will, go through all of the above at different times in your experience. It's almost like the stages of grief. You can go into denial, even denying Jesus His right to mess around in your life. You can get angry or bargain with Him. You can settle down to grim, resentful endurance. Or you can find hope and resolution. Until the next time! The trouble is, in this life there are so many losses, little and big. It seems your ears have just stopped ringing when there's another blast.

One day at church, I learned that my pastor was leaving our congregation for another assignment and that we would have to begin the search for a new pastor. It seems a small thing, but I was in great trouble at the time, and this pastor and his wife had been such a comfort and help to me. I remember walking across the parking lot, with my head down, thinking sadly, "Well, Lord, I can go through a lot of hollering and hand wringing and protesting, and then finally settle down and say,

'I guess You know best.' Or I can just say from the beginning, 'I guess You know best.' " So I tried to wait cheerfully to see what a blessing the new pastor would be. And sure enough, he was a blessing to the whole church and actually helped to bring about a miraculous conclusion to the troubles I had been having.

So when the dynamite of pain and difficulty sets off a mushroom cloud of destruction and panic in your life, don't look away. Because the next thing you will see is the impossible. Right out of that gash in the rock, right out of your deepest pain, living water will gush like Niagara. It will! We live in a broken world, and the water may be muddy and churning at first. It's not like it will be in heaven. But together, muddy and triumphant, Jesus and you will dig out that spring and clear it and line it with sparkling chunks of stone that you thought were useless rubble. It will be a sight to behold. Living water, the Spirit of God, right there in the middle of your once-desolate wilderness. Let me warn you: once you let Him loose in your life, it is next to impossible to get Him out again. You can do it. You can send Jesus away and dump dirt and rock into the spring until it eventually stops leaking through. But if you thought the job of opening the spring was hard, you'll find closing it off a thousand times harder. You would have to *really* want to get rid of Him.

And who would want to? You'd have to be nuts!

So now you have water. Take a drink—a hundred drinks! Take a bath! You'll find this living water overflows right off your land onto everyone else who gets close enough. Maybe they'll get excited too. If so, give them the name of your landscape Designer. Tell them the story. Would you believe you get a commission for everyone you interest in signing on this Master Gardener? I've found it to be true. Oh, the commission would be hard to put on a balance sheet, but it's there. It's there in the sparkle in His eyes and the joy in your own heart.

You'll be tempted just to bask beside your new spring, but one water source does not a garden make. Look around, and sure enough, there's the Gardener, huddled over His graph paper again. And this time He's conferring with a team of wreckers! What is it now?

DIG DEEPER

Have you invited the Holy Spirit to open His everlasting spring in your heart? If not, why not do so now?

Since He has begun to produce His thirst-quenching water in you (whether that was long ago or recently), how has your thirst changed? What are some things you used to thirst for, but no longer crave? What are some things you find yourself thirsty for now, that you never were interested in before?

When you first let the Gardener in, were there some unexpected results? Were there cliffs you thought were important, but that He blew out of your life? If so, have you learned to be grateful for that? Were there assets you thought were important, that He doesn't seem to value, and things you thought unimportant that He deems worthy of attention and development? Spend some time discussing these issues with Him. Try to be more aware of His work in your daily life. One way to do both is to write about them in your journal.

When were some times in your life that you have either turned Jesus away (or were tempted to), tried to argue Him into seeing things your way, hid your head and endured, or clung to Him in trust and tried to enter into His plans? Which of those times bring you the greatest joy as you recall them?

Whom will you tell this week about your Master Gardener, and how will you try to pique their interest in hiring Him for themselves?

Snapshots From My Garden

A long, long time passed. The banging of the sledgehammer echoed in her head, and most of the time she cried. Sometimes the Gardener stopped to hold and comfort her. Finally, all that ringed her world was a pile of rubble nearly hidden by a cloud of choking dust. The light was so bright now that she couldn't see, and she shivered in the breeze that had been set loose.

"Here," said the Gardener. "Try these." Out of His pack, He produced a set of strong, warm work clothes like His own. She hesitated, but much to her shame and embarrassment, the Gardener tenderly removed her old rags, bathed her in the new pool, and dressed her in the new clothes. Then He burned the old ones.

"Now you are ready to help Me," said the Gardener. "We must clear away all the rubble. Some of it we will use in our new wall. We'll use some to build up our spring and some to build the culvert under the wall at the outlet. Some is not usable and will be hauled away."

Little by little, as more time passed, she learned to fetch and carry for the Master. Together, they chose pieces of stone that sparkled or had colored markings to put around the rim of the spring. She had never known there were any beautiful stones in her wall, but in the sunlight, the new spring became her favorite place to sit.

The work was never over. They built a channel for the overflow from the spring, and a conduit for it to go out under the new wall. People—she had always dreaded people—came to see where the water was coming from, and to thank her! She stammered, "Not me, Him!" and pointed. The Gardener even hired some of the new neighbors to help them work. She found there were people who loved her, and began to love them too.

As it went up, the new wall was a source of breathless delight to her. The Gardener had brought in a whole truckload of lapis lazuli, royal blue with streaks of gold, like a palace! Carefully, using a plumb line and levels, He laid the foundation all around her garden and began to build a jeweled wall with a ruby-encrusted guard tower. She had never imagined anything so lovely and couldn't help wondering if she would be fit to live here. Was it still her home?

The plants, at least, were happy. They were growing strong and green, and the Tree lifted its branches as if it were singing to the sky. Birds even came. But she was nervous, especially when she saw Him fitting a gate of clear crystal. It was bad enough for the wall to be so low, but a crystal gate would mean people could see in! She was very uncomfortable about that.

In the evenings, all alone, they sat together by the spring or in the big canopied swing He had hung in the Tree. Wrapping His warm arm around her, the Gardener told her, "Don't be afraid. You will always be safe here, because it is no longer just your home; it is Mine. I am establishing Myself here, and no one will oppress you or make you afraid anymore. Terror won't even cross your path. If someone does try to frighten or hurt you, it will not be from Me, and they will fail, because you live with Me.

"You need a home that is open and airy. Your plants—and you, too—need sunshine, rain, and fresh air. You will find that our new garden will begin to bless all the other people around you, as well. One thing you must understand. People will be able to see in a little way, and you will be able to invite them into the gate area and tell them as much as you want about your garden, but here inside, in the secret garden, only you and I will ever come. In this world, it is not possible for people to completely share their innermost gardens. If you ever decide you wish to share your garden with another, for your whole life, then we will build adjoining gardens, and you will be able to look over the walls and learn as much as you can about each other's secret gardens, but you will never really see inside. Not here."

She felt safer then and yet strangely disappointed too. She wouldn't want anyone else all the way in here, would she? "Never?" she asked.

"Not here," He repeated. "But someday. Somewhere else, where it is always safe."

Secure in His arms, she slept.

For further insights, see Isaiah 54.

CHAPTER 4

Walls and Watchtowers: The Master's Mysterious Masonry

Another of the painful actions the Master Gardener usually begins to carry out early in the relationship is to tear down your strongholds. No matter who you are or what your past has been, you have strongholds in your life. If you have never tried to follow Him before, then pretty much everything will have to go. He is making you a whole new garden, not remodeling the old one. Remember that before this, fear or anger or mere survival has governed your life.

Judges 6:1, 2 gives a good picture of this situation. "Then the sons of Israel did what was evil in the sight of the Lord; and the Lord gave them into the hands of Midian seven years. And the power of Midian prevailed against Israel. Because of Midian the sons of Israel made for themselves the dens which were in the mountains and the caves and the strongholds." Does that sound familiar? Have you done what was evil in the sight of the Lord and had the power of your sins take over your life? Have you made dens and strongholds for yourself and hidden away in them? If so, have they succeeded in keeping you safe? Obviously not, or you wouldn't have turned to this new Gardener. Don't worry, He's going to build you some beautiful new walls. But first, the old ones have to go. And I won't try to tell you it's not scary.

I have two friends who are going through this process right now. Both of them have been in bondage to chemical addictions for years. Both have tried all the escapes they can find. Unfortunately, there was always a strong part of them that wanted to hide in those cold, deadly stone walls more than it wanted to be free. And none of their escape or control methods worked, anyway. The other day, one of them said to me with a grin, "You keep trying the same things, over and over, believing somehow you'll get different results. Somehow, *this* time it will work!" It's such a familiar attitude. And it's so stupid—after you're sane, that is.

Both of my friends have decided to surrender to the Master Gardener—really surrender. Now they're finding walls being torn down in their lives. They've lost jobs, children, families. They've lost the trust of others. I don't mean that these are things they lost only in the dark years. Some of these things they're losing now! It doesn't seem fair, does it? It doesn't seem like God's will. They finally turn themselves completely over to Him, and in comes the fleet of bulldozers! My friends are clinging to Him and to all the human hands they can too. But it's scary!

What they didn't know, and are learning now, is that God has also been building His new walls in their lives already. Those who loved them were praying the promises of Hosea over their lives. Hosea tells about someone running from God. He records God's pledge: " 'Therefore, behold, I will hedge up her way with thorns, and I will build a wall against her so that she cannot find her paths. And she will pursue her lovers [those destructive sins that imprison her], but she will not overtake them; and she will seek them, but will not find them. Then she will say, "I will go back to my first husband [God], for it was better for me then than now!" ' " (Hosea 2:6, 7). " 'Therefore, behold, I will allure her, bring her into the wilderness, and speak kindly to her. Then I will give her her vineyards from there, and the valley of Achor [trouble or affliction] as a door of hope. And she will sing there as in the days of her youth' " (verses14, 15). Ask my friends. They'll tell you this beautiful promise is true.

In some ways, this tearing-down process may be even harder to bear if you have been a faithful Christian already, trying to follow Him, building what you thought He wanted in your life. If you've just now finally let Him in and decided once and for all that *He* is the Gardener and that the garden is His, not yours, then you may be appalled to discover that pretty much everything still has to go! The best righteousness we can come up with is still filthy rags compared to His. Or in terms of our imagery, our best gardening—and I mean our very best, most loving, well-intentioned work—resembles mud pies with plastic flowers stuck in the top. " 'My thoughts are not your thoughts, neither are your ways My ways,' declares the Lord. 'For as the heavens are higher than the earth, so are My ways higher than your ways, and My thoughts than your thoughts' " (Isaiah 55:8, 9).

Does God tear down the walls even of His faithful children? Take a look at Psalm 89. This is a psalm of Ethan the Ezrahite. Ethan has a problem, and he's taking it right to the top. He is a man of faith, so he begins and ends with praise, showing that he realizes God knows what He's doing, even though Ethan himself has no clue. In the middle of the psalm, we get to the meat of the matter. In verses 19-37, Ethan recites the covenant, using God's words—"Follow Me and obey Me, and I will take care of you forever." Then Ethan wails to God, "Thou hast cast off and rejected . . . been full of wrath . . . spurned the covenant. . . . *Thou hast broken down all his walls; Thou hast brought his strongholds to ruin*" (verses 38-40, emphasis supplied). "How long, O Lord?" he asks desperately (verse 46.) Read the whole psalm for yourself. Have you ever been where Ethan is? You're blindly praising God, you're clinging to His promises, but it seems as if He's tearing you apart. Why?

I've known dedicated pastors who have worked so hard to do God's work that they've practically killed themselves. Literally. When they finally came to a skidding stop, flat on their backs, and gave the gardens of their souls wholly to the Master Gardener, some have even lost their vocations as pastors! How can that be? "Unless the Lord builds the house, they labor in vain who build it" (Psalm 127:1). It's still in vain, even if they tried to build it for Him.

The walls you've worked so hard on have to go. They are blocking out sunlight and air and maybe even the water of the Holy Spirit. Second Corinthians 10:3-5 defines some of the strongholds that may be imprisoning, instead of protecting, us. "Though we walk in the flesh, we do not war according to the flesh, for the weapons of our warfare are not of the flesh, but divinely powerful for the destruction of fortresses. We are destroying speculations and every lofty thing raised up against the knowledge of God, and we are taking every thought captive to the obedience of Christ."

Let's look a little more closely at this list.

"We are destroying speculations." I just turned to my trusty dictionary, and you'll never guess what I found! This word, *speculation,* comes from the Latin *specula,* which means watchtower! *"Speculate*: 1. to think about the various aspects of a given subject; meditate; ponder; esp. to conjecture. 2. to buy or sell stocks, commodities, land, etc., . . . or to take part in any risky venture on the chance of making huge profits." Other versions of the Bible translate this word as "imaginations." The Greek term is *logismos,* which includes the concepts of computation, reasoning, conscience, conceit, imagination, and thought.

So what does it mean to "destroy speculations"? Is God throwing down reasoning? Surely not! He is the One who made us able, like Himself, to think and choose. "Like Himself" . . . there's the rub! Is He, perhaps, throwing down *my* reasoning? Quite likely! My reasoning is the most dangerous when it comes closest to the truth. Anybody would admit that almost-truth is more dangerous than falsehood.

I think there are some clues in the above dictionary definitions—words such as *profit, conjecture, risk,* and *conceit.* The bottom line is that although God created us in His image, that image has been marred by sin, and sin is so ever-present in us, so much a part of our natures now, that our first and last real instinct is self-preservation. So our thoughts and imaginings, our best reasoning, all lean toward ways to serve our wishes, our desires—to preserve, above all, our*selves.* Or what we think of as ourselves. Actually, deep inside, in that hidden garden, there is a real self we don't even know. Jesus is seeking to recreate that true self, but first He has to destroy the false one. That's what Paul meant by dying daily. It seems like death, and it feels like death, but the end thereof—to reverse the well-known passage—is life (see Proverbs 16:25).

"We are destroying . . . every lofty thing raised up against the knowledge of God." Left to themselves, this is what our imagination and reasoning, become—lofty things raised up against the knowledge of God. Sometimes these strongholds are raised deliberately. You may have experienced that in the form of atheism, agnosticism, secular humanism, or whatever other "ism" you once used to hide from God. We're talking here about the sort of thinking that says, "Religion is the opiate of the masses." "It is illogical to believe there is a higher being, outside of and above yourself, who cares anything at all about you."

More commonly, however, these strongholds—like the chemical addictions of my friends or simple busyness and inattention to life's realities—are raised against the knowledge of God, not deliberately, exactly . . . but knowingly. We know it's wrong, and we plan to change it . . . one of these days.

Most commonly, perhaps, strongholds are raised in God's name, with good intentions. But they actually work *against* the knowledge of God. These can be good works, a religious life, even Bible knowledge. The question is: Who has built the stronghold—God Himself or a human? And the truth is, you may honestly not know. Fortunately, He does! And once you give Him permission to be your Master Designer, you'll learn a lot of shocking things just by watching what He pulls down, or allows to be pulled down, in your life.

"We are taking every thought captive to the obedience of Christ." Thoughts are great things once they're captivated by Jesus. Notice an interesting concept here. This verse is not talking about our obedience *to* Christ, though clearly that will be one result of this experience. No, the text says that our thoughts are to be captivated by the obedience *of* Christ. Think of it! *His* perfect, hard-won obedience. No mistakes. No try, try again. No half-hearted attempts. I become His, so He's mine! Awesome!

Ethan may have had tears running down his face when he wrote the last verse of Psalm 89, but he *knew* it was true. "Blessed be the Lord forever! Amen and Amen" (verse 52). Hold that verse in your heart. Like Ethan, hang on and keep watching. The next thing will be yet another miracle. Before your wondering eyes, the Master Gardener and His crew of architects will build a new wall of such beauty, of such impregnable strength, that you will begin to see your old walls and towers for the ugly, haphazard attempts they really were.

Once upon a dark, dark day, I lay half on my knees and half across my bed, weeping, trying not to let my little ones hear me. I had just learned that my husband wanted a divorce, and the psalm that came to my mind was Psalm 46. My earth was changing, the mountain on which I had built much of my life was slipping into the heart of the sea, and its waters were roaring and foaming. After a while, I opened my swollen eyes. Across the bed I saw my Bible, open to a page all marked in blue. I pulled it closer. It was Isaiah 54. I didn't remember opening the Bible at all, nor did I have a clue when I might have highlighted the whole chapter. Here are some of the verses my blurred eyes saw. " 'The Lord has called you, like a wife forsaken and grieved in spirit, even like a wife of one's youth when she is rejected,' says your God" (verse 6). " 'O afflicted one, storm-tossed, and not comforted, behold, I will set your stones in antimony, and your foundations I will lay in sapphires. Moreover, I will make your battlements of rubies, and your gates of crystal, and your entire wall of precious stones' " (verses 11, 12).

I thought God must have come down, sat on my bed, and written that for me just at that moment. Please understand. I don't mean that God tore down my first marriage. But I believe He took those ashes and rubble and that He has been building for me, during all the ensuing years, the jeweled palace He promised. How can this new wall be a thing of such beauty? Because it is built by God Himself, with Jesus as the Chief Cornerstone.

"The Lord has disciplined me severely, but He has not given me over to death. Open to me the gates of righteousness; I shall enter through them, I shall give thanks to the Lord. This is the gate of the Lord; the righteous will enter through it. I shall give thanks to Thee, for Thou hast answered me; and Thou hast become my salvation. The stone which the builders rejected has become the chief corner stone. This is the Lord's doing; it is marvelous in our eyes" (Psalm 118:18-23).

"In Thee, O Lord, I have taken refuge; let me never be ashamed . . . Be Thou to me a rock of strength, a stronghold to save me. For Thou art my rock and my fortress; for Thy name's sake Thou wilt lead me and guide me" (Psalm 31:1-3).

"Lead me to the rock that is higher than I. For Thou hast been a refuge for me, a tower of strength against the enemy. Let me dwell in Thy tent forever; let me take refuge in the shelter of Thy wings" (Psalm 61:2-4).

"Be Thou to me a rock of habitation, to which I may continually come; Thou hast given commandment to save me, for Thou art my rock and my fortress" (Psalm 71:3).

There is no better, safer, or more beautiful wall in all the universe. And that's not all. Before He's through, your Master Gardener will even build your life into a wall of safety for others!

" 'You will rebuild the ancient ruins; you will raise up the age-old foundations; and you will be called the repairer of the breach' " (Isaiah 58:12).

"And coming to Him as to a living stone, rejected by men, but choice and precious in the sight of God, you also, as living stones, are being built up as a spiritual house for a holy priesthood, to offer up spiritual sacrifices acceptable to God through Jesus Christ" (1 Peter 2:4, 5). Peter ought to know. He used to be a hard-drinking, hard-talking, hard-headed sailor. Then he became a bumbling, well-meaning follower, without enough faith to keep from betraying the One in all the world he loved the best. Could he ever in his wildest dreams have imagined that his acts and words would become the Living Word of God, used for millennia to guide and keep safe millions of God's children? Can you imagine that happening to you? Let Him have His way, and just watch!

Listen! Like many other gardeners, God likes to sing while He works. Can you hear Him?

> Let me sing now for my well-beloved a song
> of my beloved concerning His vineyard.
> My well-beloved had a vineyard on a fertile hill.
> And he dug it all around, removed its stones,
> And planted it with the choicest vine.
> And he built a tower in the middle of it,
> And hewed out a wine vat in it;
> Then He expected it to produce good grapes
> (Isaiah 5:1, 2).

I chose you, and appointed you, that you should go and bear fruit, and that your fruit should remain, that whatever you ask of the Father in My name, He may give to you (John 15:16).

DIG DEEPER

Did you once hide from God? If you have never consciously hidden from Him, have you hidden sometimes from work He wanted to do in you? What were some of the strongholds you tried to build for yourself?

Have there been strongholds He's torn out of your life, or allowed to be torn from you, that shocked and frightened you? How has He helped you to deal with this? What are you learning in the process?

Go through Psalm 89 in detail and spend prayerful time studying the progression of emotions and the growth of faith that Ethan went through. If he is in so much pain and sorrow, why does Ethan begin and end with praise? Have you learned to do that? If not, how can you develop that ability? This would be a good journal exercise.

What new protective walls and watchtowers is God building in your life? Are these visible to others or only to you? How have they made a difference to you and to those around you?

How do you visualize God as a tower or stronghold? What does it mean to you that He is your strong Fortress?

Snapshots From My Garden

Her life was far different than it had ever been before. She had always valued her privacy, and she was still uncomfortable with the people who came to look over her walls, ask questions, and give advice. But she could sometimes talk to them now. Some of their advice was good, and once or twice she even answered a question herself.

She was always busy. She had planted her few plants, still rather spindly, in a bit of ground near the corner of a wall, and she had to carry water to them, dust their leaves, and watch for bugs. More important, she helped with the cleanup and wall-building when she could. And, of course, there was always the Tree to tend. The grim darkness in which she had existed before was receding into the dimness of memory, but her most valued possession from those days—self-sufficiency—was still with her. She had been a whole world to herself then. She had prided herself on the fact that no matter how bad it got, she had never begged for help.

She had kept busy then too. There had been spiders to chase, holes to patch, and always the two overriding passions—care of the Tree and the ongoing construction of her fortress. Safety had been her primary goal in those days—safety, secrecy, and privacy.

Now the Gardener had shown her that she could be safe if He was around, even if the wall was only a low one. It was a little unnerving, but on the whole, nice. The sunshine was warm, and the fresh air made her feel stronger than she had felt in years. She had learned to love the water.

Yet, in some ways, things were not all that different. The main goals of life hadn't changed. The Tree was still all, and the construction of the wall still ongoing. Her garden was still hers to care for. Well, with the Gardener's help, of course. She could never be grateful enough for all He had done. Still, she didn't need to bother Him for every little thing.

So the days passed, and though the Gardener was always around somewhere, she didn't often see much of Him. She heard Him—busy with some facet of construction or murmuring over His endless plans—and knew He was there. That was enough. Once she thought she heard Him call her name, but she was busy. And when she looked around a minute later, He wasn't there. It must have been her imagination.

Then, early one morning, when the shadow of the growing watchtower lay long across the garden, she came around the Tree and was surprised to see the Gardener sitting alone in the swing, looking—well, looking almost sad! She was so surprised she stopped and stared. She had never seen Him sad before.

Then He looked up and saw her, and His whole face lit up.

"You came!" He said.

"I . . . I . . . What are You doing?"

"Waiting for you," said the Gardener.

"But . . . did we have an appointment?"

"I've been calling you every morning, but you didn't seem to hear."

"Oh! I'm sorry, but I've been busy, You know . . . Did You want something?"

"Just to sit with you. I've been missing you."

"Missing me? I've been here all along!"

"So have I," said the Gardener quietly. "Will you sit with Me?"

"Well, I do have a lot to do right now. I know! Why don't You come and work with me, and we can talk at the same time?"

"No," said the Gardener. "I want you to sit here with Me."

He was beginning to look sad again, so she said, "All right, if it's so important to You, but only for a few minutes." She perched beside Him in the swing, feeling a little anxious to be about her business, and even, just slightly, irritated. Then she felt guilty. What right did she have to be irritated with Him of all people—the One who had saved her life and was building her a whole new garden.

"I can never be grateful enough to You," she said awkwardly, "for all You've done and everything. I wish there were some way I could pay You back." It was a useless statement, and she knew it. How could she ever begin to pay Him back?

The Gardener looked at her. "Thank you," He said gravely. "There is something I want from you."

She swallowed. Here it came. She had known all along it was too good to be true. "What's that?"

"I want you to sit here with Me in the sun."

She looked at Him. "And?"

"Just sit here with Me. We can talk or plan or sometimes just sit in the sun. You need more sun."

She started to protest and then realized she had, in fact, been keeping to the shadows much of the time, even in her work. Old habits died hard. Well, she could sit in the sun. But she was still confused. "That's all You want?"

"Every day," He said.

"Every day! But I—we—have so much to . . ."

"Every day," He repeated. His gaze held hers for a minute—or longer. His eyes always made her want to do anything He asked.

"All right. Every day."

He touched her face and smiled. The sun seemed suddenly brighter.

CHAPTER 5

Climate Considerations—1: The Sun of Righteousness

What is the biggest paradox in gardening? Weather! It's the single most important factor, the one without which your garden can't survive, and the one over which you have absolutely no control. That's a surefire recipe for frustration!

So what's a gardener to do? Try to control the uncontrollable, of course. Build a cold frame, a hotbed, a greenhouse! Set up a sprinkler or an irrigation system. Put screens and shades over delicate plants. Install an expensive ventilation system in the greenhouse.

Unless you've chosen to contract with the Master Gardener Himself. As soon as He arrives on the scene, all your work, seen in the light of His knowing eyes, will suddenly seem cheap, shoddy, ugly, and worthy only of speedy destruction. You'll learn, as we saw in the last chapter, that what you saw as necessary protection was really just a prison, keeping out more than it kept in. The Gardener will assure you that what you need most is untrammeled access to all the fresh air, sunshine, and rain you can get, and He'll tear everything down. The result of this wholesale revolution will be to leave you standing, blinking and exposed, in the full glare of more light than you've ever experienced.

But don't be afraid. The Bible says, "The Lord God is a sun *and* a shield," and He "gives [both] grace and glory" (Psalm 84:11, emphasis supplied). He will give you only what you can stand.

Up to now, this book has concentrated on the work of God in our lives. All we've had to do—all we have been able to do—is cooperate. Or not. God chose a garden site—you. He asked you if He could build a new creation in you, and you said Yes. He opened a spring in you, the indwelling presence of His Holy Spirit, and began to develop it. He began breaking ground for future construction, tearing down your strongholds and putting in His own beautiful walls, hedges, and guard towers for your protection. Instead of resisting Him, you've tried to learn to take joy and hope in what He does in you, even when it hurts. But there hasn't been much *you* could do. This is the chapter where the change begins. Here and throughout the rest of the book we will learn some practical things *we* can do as caretakers of our own souls. We will also continue to learn and relearn, over and over, that even when we are working under His direction, *He* is still really doing the work *in* us.

We'll start with the primary source of energy—the sun. Plant and animal life would not exist if it weren't for the sun, and the garden that doesn't get enough sunshine will not thrive as it should. In terms of our analogy, the sun is God's presence, and our first and most essential duty as caretakers is not the work we do in our gardens, but simply time spent sitting in the sun. It seems strange and counter-intuitive, and some of us take a lifetime to learn it, but it's the first thing the Master Gardener asks us to do.

Every day—*every* day—first thing out of bed, we need to spend some time just sitting and basking in the light of His presence. Here is where some people do their heavy-duty study. I can't. If you can, be sure you don't let study take the place of basking. Reading His words, especially the Bible passages where Jesus is speaking, or some of Isaiah, the Psalms, or any passage where you hear His voice, is one great way to converse with God. But serious study, although very important, is not the same. We can never get enough time just sitting at His feet and soaking in the reality of His incredible love, His inexhaustible patience, His unfathomable sacrifice. . . . Notice how language begins to fail when we try to describe the experience. Be there. Feel His arms around you. Hear His whispers. Touch the face of God. Taste of His goodness. And smell the perfume of heaven, through doors God has left ajar.

Another way to take in God's sunshine is in the dazzling light of new truth or a truth that's new to you or a new facet of an old and beloved truth. This is where study and sermons and church and books and radio or TV programs come in. " 'For you who fear My name the sun of righteousness will rise with healing in its wings; and you will go forth and skip about like calves from the stall' " (Malachi 4:2). Have you ever seen calves, lambs, or kids just released from stalls into fields full of sunshine and clover? They leap and bounce and gallop as if the world were just that minute invented for them alone. I can personally attest that new light from God can have that same effect.

I was eighteen when I sat in a camp-meeting pavilion in Ohio and heard Pastors Joel Thompkins and Morris Venden explain salvation by grace alone in language I could understand. My mother was with me, and we literally held hands and skipped from the pavilion that day. People looked at us a little strangely. Maybe they already understood and didn't catch the excitement. Actually, it's slightly embarrassing to remember now.

Of course, I realized later that many preachers had been preaching the same thing all along. But they hadn't said it in *our* language—my mother's and mine—I guess. It was new to us, and oh the joy! The incredible relief! You mean we could give up our endless, desperate, hopeless slogging through the quicksand of Never Quite Good Enough and live in the sunshine? You mean we could eat green grass and grow strong, instead of trying somehow to make ourselves strong enough to deserve green grass? You mean we could splash in the rain of the Holy Spirit and really get clean, instead of hiding from the rain and washing over and over in the same muddy bucket? You mean . . . ? WHOOPEEEE!!!!! HALLELUJAH!!!!!

Now here's an interesting paradox about spiritual weather. The light we had encountered before had been only frightening. All it did was show us how dirty we were, and all that accomplished was to increase our sense of guilt and unworthiness. I think the difference was that before, we had seen light as individual truths (doctrines) or as the Scriptures (Thy Word is a lamp unto my path), but now God's spokesmen were showing us Jesus Himself as the Light. Pastor Venden, for example, would be the first to tell you that his best knowledge, his best theories, his best writing, held up to illuminate someone's path, would be as useless as a flashlight without batteries. It's Jesus who does the lighting. In fact, it's Jesus who is the Light.

Our experience—my mother's and mine—exemplifies the truth that the light of God has different effects on different people at different times. The Bible says that "the people who walk in darkness will see a great light; those who live in a dark land, the light will shine on them" (Isaiah 9:2). And Matthew makes it clear that this light is offered to all: " 'Your Father who is in heaven . . . causes His sun to rise on the evil and the good' " (5:45). Yet John tells of two kinds of people for whom the light does little or no good. Speaking of Jesus as the Light, John says, "The light shines in the darkness, and the darkness did not comprehend it" (John 1:5). This had happened to my mother and me, and it happens to many other sincere seekers. We had not knowingly refused any of God's light, but we had not comprehended it, so we were still in darkness in some important ways. Luckily, God never gives up, and over the years, He had done a lot of invisible preparatory work—torn down a lot of our self-protective strongholds—to prepare us to stand in the light and see clearly that year at camp meeting.

Then, John speaks of those who refuse God's light: "There was the true light which, coming into the world, enlightens every man. He was in the world, and the world was made through Him, and the world did not know Him. He came to His own, and those who were His own did not receive Him" (John 1:9-11).

This is very dangerous ground indeed. Isaiah 50:11 contains God's warning to those who reject His light and walk instead in their own light. This includes those who walk in the light kindled by other humans, without studying for themselves under the direct training of the Holy Spirit. "Behold, all you who kindle a fire, who encircle yourselves with firebrands, walk in the light of your fire and among the brands you have set ablaze. This you will have from My hand; and you will lie down in torment" (Isaiah 50:11). In other words, like any father, God will make you regret your waywardness, in the desperate hope He can get you to look to Him after all. If you doubt that, read the next verse— and remember that the Bible didn't originally have chapter breaks. " '*Listen* to me, you who pursue righteousness . . . : Look to the rock from which you were hewn' " (Isaiah 51:1, emphasis supplied). There's more, and it turns to gardening, too. Be sure to read it all for yourself.

The story of Pharaoh shows clearly how the sun of righteousness affects someone who determinedly continues to reject it. Just as the same sun melts wax, but hardens clay, so God's acts softened the hearts of many and added an unnumbered "mixed multitude" to the throng of Israel that left Egypt. But His same acts hardened Pharaoh's heart until it was like granite. God forbid any of us should ever be found in that condition!

Prevent it by diligently studying, seeking to know the Bible backward and forward and inside out for yourself. Know the truths of God's doctrines. Know the truths of the prophetic timetables. Know the stories of those who did—and did not—walk in God's light. When you are shown something you have been seeing in the wrong light or haven't seen at all, ask God for the humility to accept it willingly from His hand and make the necessary changes, whether in your attitudes or in your actions. (Usually both!)

Because "as many as received Him, to them He gave the right to become children of God" (John 1:12). " 'While you have the light, believe in the light, in order that you may become sons of light.... I have come as light into the world, that everyone who believes in Me may not remain in darkness' " (John 12:36, 46). Let's pray daily that we will never want anything more than we want to be children of God and children of light.

There's still another way to let more light into our lives. Jesus says, " 'I am the light of the world; he who *follows* Me shall not *walk* in the darkness, but shall have the light of life' " (John 8:12, emphasis supplied). Once we learn to spend time *every day* basking in God's presence, once we learn to listen carefully to Him and love and accept the truths He shows us, the inner gardens of our souls will be so full of sunlight and warmth that they will begin to spill over into other gardens nearby. We will be equipped to do the works of light, with God. What are those, exactly?

"This is the message we have heard from Him and announce to you, that God is light, and in Him there is no darkness at all. If we say that we have fellowship with Him and yet walk in the darkness, we lie and do not practice the truth; but if we walk in the light as He Himself is in the light, we *have fellowship with one another*, and the blood of Jesus His Son cleanses us from all sin" (1 John 1:5-7, emphasis supplied). "The darkness is passing away, and the true light is already shining. The one who says he is in the light and yet hates his brother is in the darkness until now. The *one who loves his brother abides in the light* and there is no cause for stumbling in him" 1 John 2:8-10, emphasis supplied).

Here, John defines walking in the light, as opposed to walking in the darkness. Love is light; hatred is darkness, which makes sense if God is the Light and God is Love. So walking in the light means loving others. And according to the Sermon on the Mount, it includes even the ability to love those who hate us!

I can speak for myself, that when I used to (and when I sometimes still do) hide out in the secret strongholds I made in my soul for "safety," although I wasn't acting in a knowingly hateful way, I was thinking only of myself and my emotional safety. I didn't think of others and their needs, but only of how they were threats to my self or at least to my self-image. It didn't make me feel any safer, I might add. I always had to burrow deeper and ever deeper, but still the fear was there.

Fear is the other opposite of love that John cites (see 1 John 4:18). When Jesus came in and broke down my strongholds, when He taught me to sit with Him, to listen to Him, He made me able to really see others, and even to love them in my own childish imitation of His love for me.

What is the result of all this walking around in Jesus-light? "A great sign appeared in heaven: a woman [that's the church—you and me!] *clothed with the sun*" (Revelation 12:1, emphasis supplied). Imagine! All wrapped up in His light! Jesus says, " 'The righteous will shine forth as the sun in the kingdom of their Father. He who has ears, let him hear' " (Matthew 13:43).

Believe it or not, we—yes, you and I—will shine with the reflected glory of the Sun of Righteousness! And it will be noticed. " 'Arise, shine; for your light has come, and the glory of the Lord has risen upon you.... And nations will come to your light, and kings to the brightness of your rising. Lift up your eyes round about, and see; they all gather together, they come to you. Your sons will come from afar, and your daughters will be carried in the arms. Then you will see and be radiant, and your heart will thrill and rejoice ... for the name of the Lord your God, and for the Holy One of Israel because He has glorified you' " (Isaiah 60:1- 9). So, " 'let your light shine before men in such a way that they may see your good works, and glorify your Father who is in heaven' " (Matthew 5:16).

Then all His other wandering, cold, scared children will flock to the light, and together we'll shine all the way to heaven. "The city has no need of the sun or of the moon to shine upon it, for the glory of God has illumined it, and its lamp is the Lamb. And the nations shall walk by its light, and the kings of the earth shall bring their glory into it" (Revelation 21:23, 24). "And there shall no longer be any night; and they shall not have need of the light of a lamp nor the light of the sun, because the Lord God shall illumine them; and they shall reign forever and ever" (Revelation 22:5).

Forever and ever! And it all began the day we let the Master Gardener tear down our strongholds and shine His love all over us. It continues as we learn to simply be in His presence. To live and move and have our being in Him and practice being aware of Him. It includes prayer, meditation, Bible study, church, and other services, but it doesn't require any particular action or method. Just be with Him and be aware of Him. It sounds so simple, doesn't it? But it requires eternal vigilance and practice. After a while, our hearts will turn to Him all the time, as naturally as a flower follows the sun, and then we'll know the Gardener is really at work.

DIG DEEPER

In the "snapshot" appearing before this chapter, our caretaker had become so busy doing what seemed to her to be right, that she forgot to allow the Master Gardener to teach her *His* priorities. Think or write about times you have found yourself doing that. What are the priorities to which you tend to give the most attention? What is Jesus' number one priority for you? How can you get in His way without even meaning to—and what can you do to correct and prevent it?

How and when do you bask in the sunlight of God's presence? Do you need to set aside more time for this? (Most of us do!)

In what ways has God been a "sun" to you, showing you new light you had never seen before?

In what ways has He been a "shield" to you, shading you from the glare of light that was too much for you at the time?

Have you ever let His light harden you instead of melting you? What can you do about that? *Warning: The answer is, NOTHING! You can only turn yourself over, wholeheartedly and without reservation, to Him. He is the One who takes away the stony heart and gives you a whole new one, that will melt in His presence, instead of becoming stone throughout.* If you ever, now or in the future, find yourself hardening, you are in danger, and must immediately turn yourself to Him, ask Him for repentance, and lay bare your heart with all its dark corners, for His inspection and correction.

How and when do you do deep, searching Bible study? Do you do enough? Do you tend to follow others' thinking, or conversely, to be too stubborn in your own opinions? How can you be sure to follow neither of these extremes?

How have you seen more love and obedience in your life as a result of following Jesus and walking in His light? In what areas of your life do you pray for still more love?

Using your best imagination, write in your journal what you think it will be like when we reflect perfectly the light of God's face in heaven and live always in light that would be unbearably strong for us now.

Snapshots From My Garden

She was working when the water began to fall from the sky. First the sun had gone away. Now that she was used to the bright light, it was a little frightening to have it suddenly disappear. But she had lived in much deeper darkness, so she looked around nervously and just kept working. Then she felt the first drop.

Startled, she looked up, and more drops fell on her head and face and arms. The wind was blowing, so the wetness made her shiver. Then the sky seemed to cave in and fall on her in a great rush of cold and wet. With a cry of fear, she ran for shelter. But where could she run? There was no shelter such as she had been used to before. Just a low wall and the watchtower, still under construction. She heard a noise above the sound of the wind and water and ran frantically in circles until she came to a stop, shivering miserably, under the branches of her Tree.

The noise came again. She realized, suddenly, that it was the Gardener, calling her name. "Here!" she wailed.

His face appeared between the leaves, smiling (rather heartlessly, she thought crossly) at her predicament. "Why are you hiding? Come out."

"No! It's wet! What's happening? Make it stop!" She had grown enough to know that she sounded like a spoiled child, and she felt a little ashamed, which made her more cross than ever.

The Gardener still smiled. Water was running down His face and off His beard. He held out a wet hand. "Come. It's rain. It won't hurt you. In fact, your garden will die without it. Come on. I'll show you."

It was becoming daily more important to her to do anything He asked her to, but this was too much. "No," she pouted, huddling closer against the rough bark of the Tree.

"Yes. Come." The Gardener reached into her hideout and possessed Himself of one of her hands. "I'll put My cloak over you."

Reluctantly, and not without whimpering, she allowed herself to be pulled out of her shelter and into the shelter of His arm and His cloak. She felt immediately warmer and safer, and some of the fear faded. He led her around to the other side of the Tree, where the water came out. "See?" He pointed to the little pool they had made for the spring. "The level was getting low. You needed this rain."

"I thought You said there was enough to last forever."

"There is. It's kept in the Father's storehouse of the clouds. He sends it when it's needed, so that you will always have a bountiful supply. Come and see how your plants like it."

Slowly, they toured the garden, which was still pretty bare, but was beginning to look as if it might be pretty and useful someday. As she saw the thirsty gratitude of her few plants, she began to realize what a blessing the rain really was. She still didn't like it, but she decided she could live with it—once in a while. She apologized to the Gardener for her attitude.

"You've decided you can bear it?" He asked with a grin. "Once in a while, anyway?"

She stared. It wasn't enough that He was always talking her into things she didn't really want to do—now He could read her mind?

The Gardener laughed. "You've just begun," He assured her. "You will learn to rejoice in the rain and to sing and dance with Me in it." She shook her head emphatically. She couldn't even imagine it. "Yes, you will." He drew her close under His cloak. "But not yet. Sit with Me in our swing, watch the silver drops fall, and listen to their music. Just as I asked you to spend time with Me in the sunshine, so I want you to spend time with Me in the rain."

As they settled into their canopied tree swing, He laughed again and added, "At least you can't make the excuse that you have work to do!"

She couldn't help smiling. From within His cloak and under a canopy, the rain did seem almost silver.

CHAPTER 6

Climate Considerations—2: Showers of Blessing

Warm and comforting and good for basking as it is, sunshine by itself will not make you grow. You need rain too. Your garden has already been broken open to receive the Holy Spirit within, but rain must fall on your life from the outside, too.

" 'Let us know, let us press on to know the Lord. His going forth is as certain as the dawn; and He will come to us like the rain, like the spring rain watering the earth' " (Hosea 6:3). If sunshine is a good image of the warm, comforting, all-pervading presence of God, rain is a good image of His nurturing. If we "press on to know the Lord," He will "come to us like the rain." God says through the prophet Ezekiel, " 'I will cause showers to come down in their season; they will be showers of blessing' " (Ezekiel 34:26).

It all sounds so cozy, so refreshing, like a gentle April shower that brings May flowers. Sometimes it is. But just as often, it isn't especially comfortable. God's nurturing, by definition, includes His teaching and training, and that can be downright scary. In Psalm 68 David recounts, in figurative language, the story of God giving His law at Sinai: "The earth quaked; the heavens also dropped rain at the presence of God;

Sinai itself quaked at the presence of God, the God of Israel" (verse 8). It sounds scary, and we know from the story in Exodus that the people were so frightened that they asked Moses to talk to them for God from then on—they didn't want to hear from God Himself. Yet God was only trying to teach them how to love Him and be His children. David goes on in verses 9 and 10, "Thou didst shed abroad a plentiful rain, O God; Thou didst confirm Thine inheritance, when it was parched. Thy creatures settled in it; Thou didst provide in Thy goodness for the poor, O God." So to David, God's presence, bringing His law (the description of His character), is like rain that relieves parched land and makes a place for His creatures to settle comfortably and be at peace.

Here's a "rain" story from my younger days. Those who know me will find this shocking, but I was an agonizingly shy child. Away from home, I never spoke unless spoken to, and not comfortably then. So imagine my horror one Sabbath to discover that the previous week my class at church had taken advantage of my absence to choose me as a speaker at an upcoming youth rally! To this day I don't know why. I suspect because they couldn't get enough willing volunteers!

I was fourteen years old, possibly the most fragile age in the human life span. I lived in Seattle, and the rally would be held in a large coliseum. It was expected there would be thousands in attendance. I was so upset I cried right in class in front of everybody, which was the next worse thing after death. But they wouldn't let me off the hook. "I know you can do it," said my teacher.

When I got home, I decided to enlist my mother. She would tell them I didn't have to do it. But my own mother betrayed me. She, too, thought I could do it. In fact, she thought that the point wasn't even what I could or couldn't do. "The words aren't yours, they're God's," she told me. And she showed me this passage: " 'For My thought are not your thoughts, neither are your ways My ways,' declares the Lord. " 'For as the heavens are higher than the earth, so are My ways higher than your ways, and My thoughts than your thoughts. For as the rain and the snow come down from heaven, and do not return there without watering the earth, and making it bear and sprout, and furnishing seed to the sower and bread to the eater; so shall My word be which goes forth from My mouth; it shall not return to Me empty, without accomplishing what I desire, and without succeeding in the matter for which I sent it' " (Isaiah 55:9-11).

"So you see," said Mother, "it's God's Word, and it's entirely His responsibility how people receive it or whether they listen or what it accomplishes. All you have to do is present it the very best you can."

"All?" I wailed. "That's the hard part! I just can't! I'll be too scared!"

Mother went on to the rest of the passage: " 'For you will go out with joy, and be led forth with peace; the mountains and the hills will break forth into shouts of joy before you, and all the trees of the field will clap their hands' " (verse 12).

"That's the part of the promise that is for you," said Mother. "God will lead you forth onto that platform with peace. I'll be praying and claiming that promise for you."

So I was stuck. I read the mini-sermon provided for me and began to be intrigued. I thought I would have liked to write my own sermon.

There were 2,000 people in front of me when I spoke. At least one of them was praying for me to be led forth in peace. Probably my teacher was too. Probably the whole church was! I shook like a leaf. I thought I would fall down. I also preached God's Word. It was pretty cool, actually—after it was over.

Three years later, I volunteered to speak in a youth week of prayer. I got to write my own sermon that time. I've been speaking ever since. And that passage has gotten me through some times very much tougher than that one. So you see why it's a favorite with me, especially the last verse. " 'Instead of the thorn bush [which I often expect] the cypress will come up; and instead of the nettle [ditto] the myrtle will come up; and it will be a memorial to the Lord, for an everlasting sign which will not be cut off' " (verse 13).

That passage, and the seasons of my life that it represents, are everlasting memorials to the Lord for me. God's Word has rained into my life and watered and refreshed me, making me grow—which is always pretty cool. But sometimes only after it's over!

This story also exemplifies another biblical principle, which is that the teachings of wise people can be rain from God, too. In Moses' song of praise, recorded in Deuteronomy 32, he asks this blessing from God: " 'Let my teaching drop as the rain, my speech distill as the dew, as the droplets on the fresh grass and as the showers on the herb' " (verse 2). Do we ask that of God before we try to teach anything to anyone else? How can we be sure our words will be that kind of blessing to others? Verse 3: " 'I proclaim the Name of the Lord; ascribe greatness to our God!' "

In Psalm 72:6, Solomon asks the same blessing for himself and every king. "May he come down like rain upon the mown grass, like showers that water the earth." And again in Proverbs 16:15: "In the light of a king's face is life, and his favor is like a cloud with the spring rain." I believe these are blessings that apply to anyone in a leadership position of any kind. And I think, if we are leaders (including parents), we should pray these blessings not only for ourselves, but for *our* leaders and strive to see and accept their leadership as gratefully as our thirsty gardens drink in rain.

But what about the thunderstorms and hurricanes and blizzards in life? Is God in those? Do they have a purpose, other than destruction?

Let's look at Psalm 18, sometimes known as the "thunderstorm psalm." The whole psalm is interesting, but we'll start with verses 9-15: "He bowed the heavens also, and came down with thick darkness under His feet. And He rode upon a cherub and flew; and He sped upon the wings of the wind. He made darkness His hiding place, His canopy around Him, darkness of waters, thick clouds of the skies. From the brightness before Him passed His thick clouds, hailstones and coals of fire. The Lord also thundered in the heavens, and the Most High uttered His voice, hailstones and coals of fire. And He sent out His arrows, and scattered them [David's enemies], and lightning flashes in abundance, and routed them. Then the channels of water appeared, and the foundations of the world were laid bare at Thy rebuke, O Lord, at the blast of the breath of Thy nostrils."

Sounds terrifying, doesn't it? But keep reading. "He sent from on high, He took me; He drew me out of many waters…. The Lord was my stay. He brought me forth also into a broad place; He rescued me, because He delighted in me" (verses 16-19).

There is a rain that comes from the hand of God, bringing growth and blessing in its drops. Sometimes this is a gentle rain, and sometimes a hard one, but it is always to be received with joy and thanksgiving. Dance in it with Him!

Then there is a rain that comes only because the world is sinful and broken—rain that comes from the battle between the Creator and the "prince of the power of the air" (Ephesians 2:2) and is intended for destruction. That is, Satan intends it for the destruction of God's children, and God intends it to destroy evil and to make His wandering ones look up to Him and be saved. But if you have committed the garden of your soul to the Master Gardener, He rides on even those thunderbolts, scoops you up out of the floodwaters, and carries you with Him where you are safe.

I always thought the garden itself would be safe, as long as He was in it. I learned otherwise. He only promised that *I*—the inside I, the real I, the I that He can reconstruct even if I die—would be safe. I stood one day in my inner sanctum, turning and turning, bewildered and terrified, seeing only destruction on every hand. My garden was blackened, muddy, ruined. Smoke rose from some places. The wall and watchtower were broken, though they still stood. My life as I knew it had been destroyed. Yet here I was, limping, but alive. My Master Gardener had carried me through the storm. But He hadn't saved the garden on which we had worked so hard.

I chose not to put this experience in the snapshot allegories between these chapters, because I want to tell you in specific language exactly what I did. Many people, standing and weeping in ruins of their own, have asked me about it. First, I gave up. I withdrew into depression and anger and turned my back against Jesus and His comfort. Then the depression and sullenness changed. Rage such as I had never known began to consume me from the inside out. How could He? How *dare* He? I could, at this moment, have turned Him out and canceled His contract. If I had been a younger Christian, I might have. But He had been the center of my life always. Who else is there? What else can you do, and where else can you go to cry? Maybe, I reasoned, it was a sin to be so angry at God. But if His shoulders weren't broad enough to handle it, whose were?

So, one day when I had time to myself, I decided to go straight to the top this time. I bowed my head and prayed to be wrapped in the Holy Spirit like a blanket, like a space ship, so I could go into heaven alive. I imagined the stars flowing past us as we flew through the galaxy, through Orion's belt, to the pearly gates. The angels on guard at the gates took one look at us, at my furious and determined face, and opened the doors and got out of the way. Past the golden streets we raced, with hardly a glance—along the banks of the River, past the double-trunked Tree, through more gates, into the Throne Room of the Almighty. There was the Father, on His throne, at the center of power, in charge of the universe. There, beside Him, stood the Son. I was a little scared, having gotten this far in my imaginings. Then Father held out His arms.

I threw myself in His lap, and His arms closed around me. Jesus drew near, too, and the Spirit remained with me. I threw a royal tantrum. I cried; I screamed; I told Him exactly what I thought of what had happened to my life. I wailed that I had done exactly what He told me to do in a terribly agonizing situation, and this was my reward. I said He had—I hesitated—I said I *felt* as if He had betrayed me. He Himself, by His own hand.

He listened. It took a long time.

When my weeping had quieted to exhaustion, God said, "Give Me your anger."

I looked up at Him. I could hardly see through my swollen eyes. I knew it was one of those moments when it wasn't just my imagination anymore. "What?" I said.

"Give Me your anger."

I looked down. It was as if my anger had become a black, ugly, spiky thing in my hand. I suddenly realized how unworthy a thing that is to give to God. Besides, deep inside, something whispered that if I gave it to Him, I had to give it up. "I can't," I said.

He held out His hand and waited.

Finally, reluctantly, I turned it over to Him. For just an instant, I saw that horrible ugliness in the holiness of His hand. Then it became a shining sword. I stared. He handed it back to me, hilt first. Hesitantly, I took it.

"Anger," said my Father, "given to Me, can be a weapon for good. A weapon to change that which needs changing."

"How?" I asked.

"I'll teach you," He promised.

I opened my eyes. I was in my room. I was still alive. I still hurt. My garden was still in a shambles. I still didn't know what to do in the situation in which I found myself. But something had changed. And I had learned one of the most important lessons of my life, one of the most important things I can share with you. Not only is it OK to take your anger to God, *you must*. There is no place else in the universe where it can be dealt with. And you cannot heal or begin to learn to use it for good—"the anger of man does not achieve the righteousness of God" (James 1:20)—until you have turned it over to Him.

Over time, sooner than I expected, I saw green shoots pushing through the ashes of my inner garden. Virtues and faith grew better and stronger and faster in me because of the fertilization and plowing the ground had received. The Gardener has been teaching me ever since (I am a slow learner) how to know when to give up anger and put it aside as unworthy and unusable, and when and how to use anger for good.

So there is gentle rain, and there are horrific storms. And then there are the times when you would give anything you own for one drop. There are droughts.

Quite a few well-known Christians have written and spoken on the dry spells in their lives—times when there seems to be no rain at all even though they are still praying and still trusting. It's a good thing they have left their experiences for others to read, or I would have gotten more discouraged than I have at the droughts that have come to me. I have to assume that if these barren periods have come to Elijah and

Paul and George Mueller and Keith Miller and Joyce Landorf, they are going to come to me.

Interestingly, the Bible doesn't promise that our gardens will be protected from droughts. It says, " 'Blessed is the man who trusts in the Lord and whose trust is the Lord. For he will be like a tree planted by the water, that extends its roots by a stream and will not fear when the heat comes; but its leaves will be green, and it will not be anxious in a year of drought nor cease to yield fruit' " (Jeremiah 17:7, 8). So heat and drought will come, but we need not fear.

Speaking from experience, it will not always seem as though there is fruit, either. There have been periods of my life when Bible study and prayer felt like nothing more than a habit—a habit that was a struggle to keep up, too! There were no insights from the Lord, and growth, if any, had slowed to a crawl. During these times, it is always an astonishment to me when someone says that something I have said or done was an encouragement or a source of growth or strength to them. That's fruit. And how many times does it happen, when no one says anything to us? How many times have we learned some bit of patience or acceptance that is one of God's goals for us, and we don't even realize it?

Here is the promise, as sure as God is God: " 'The land into which you are about to cross to possess it [in our case, the new garden He is planting in you], a land of hills and valleys, drinks water from the rain of heaven, a land for which the Lord your God cares; the eyes of the Lord your God are always on it, from the beginning even to the end of the year. And it shall come about, if you listen obediently to my commandments which I am commanding you today, to love the Lord your God and to serve Him with all your heart and all your soul, that He will give the rain for your land *in its season,* the early and late rain, that you may gather in your grain and your new wine and your oil…. And you shall eat and be satisfied" (Deuteronomy 11:11-15, emphasis supplied). And as we saw at the beginning of this chapter, Ezekiel 34:26 also promises that showers of blessing will " 'come down in their season.' "

Only God really knows the seasons of your life. His eyes are always on you to bless you. When the dry times come, don't stop talking to the Gardener. Zechariah 10:1 says to "*ask* rain from the Lord at the time of the spring rain—the Lord who makes the storm clouds; and He will give them showers of rain, vegetation in the field to each [one]" (emphasis supplied). Then wait patiently. Now there's the hard part! "Be patient, therefore, brethren, until the coming of the Lord. Behold, the farmer waits for the precious produce of the soil, being patient about it, until it gets the early and late rains" (James 5:7).

What are these early and late rains that the Bible repeatedly mentions? In the warm, Middle Eastern climate, the early rains come in the fall and soften the ground for seed sowing. The latter rains come in the spring and bring the flush of growth for the harvest. In our lives, just as in the real world of agriculture, these cycles happen over and over, I believe. Just about the time you are rejoicing in one harvest, you get plowed and rained on for another seed sowing.

Like everything else, you can choose to receive God's presence, typified by nurturing rain, or not. As Hebrews 6:7, 8 points out, "For ground that drinks the rain which often falls upon it and brings forth vegetation useful to those for whose sake it is also tilled, receives a blessing from God; but if it yields thorns and thistles, it is worthless and close to being cursed, and it ends up being burned." But if you have refused God's blessing and are withering, the rain will come again, and you will get another chance. Drink it in! Rejoice in it! Dance in it with your Master Gardener! To measure your harvest, don't try to count up the good works and fruits you think you see (or don't see) in yourself. Instead, keep a watch on the shine in His eyes. That's how you'll know for sure you are growing just as He has planned.

DIG DEEPER

In your journal, write a story of a time when God's gentle nurturing rain taught you something you needed to know—and how it blessed you. Then contrast that experience with a heavy rainstorm that you feared would drown you, but that God still used for your good. How did that bless you? Have you thanked Him for those times?

When have the teachings of a wise person rained into your life and blessed you? Have you thanked him or her?

Make a list of the leaders for whom you want to pray—that their (and your) words will be like dew in the lives they touch. If you are a leader or teacher or parent, how can you be sure that your teaching is centered on God Himself, and not on your own ideas, or anyone else's ideas, *about* God?

Have you ever been totally, painfully honest with God about negative feelings you've had toward Him? Did you let Him take those feelings and do with them as He wished? If not, what's stopping you?

What are some of the ways God has been teaching you about anger management? If this is an area in which you need help, don't be afraid to look for Christian pastors or counselors who might be able to help you.

Have there been droughts in your life? How can you tell when they are of your own making and when they are just there, to be patiently endured, looking up and waiting for the rain?

Can you see in your life, both early rains near the beginning of your walk with God, and latter ones that are bringing maturity and fruit? (If you are a new Christian, just wait—I promise it will happen to you, too! In the meantime, eat and drink of Him, care for your garden, and grow as His beloved child.)

Snapshots From My Garden

She sat by herself in the swing, pushing with her feet and swinging high into the air and down again. The swing was wide, having been built for two, and she sat in the middle and stretched her arms like wings to each side to reach the ropes. Warm wind blew her hair into her face as she flew backward—and out of her face as she sailed forward. She inhaled deeply and smiled without knowing it. A rich aroma—damp earth, green things, barely visible blossoms on the Tree, and some nameless perfume—filled her to her toes with contentment.

She saw her Gardener coming toward her and dragged her feet to stop the swing. The wind blew His hair, too, and as He watched her, His face seemed to glow with joy.

"What is it?" she asked Him.

"What is what?"

She laughed. She knew He knew and that He would make her say it anyway so that she would think it through and hear herself ask clearly. "In the wind," she said, closing her eyes and sniffing. "There's . . . " She thought some more and opened her eyes. "Life," she said. "There's Life in the wind. What is it?"

His eyes crinkled. "It's Life. You have spoken more truly than you know. It is the Holy Spirit of Life. You cannot see Him or know where He goes or what He does, but I will tell you from where He comes. He comes from My Father and from Me, and when you inhale Him, you inhale Life Eternal— and exhale joy and praise."

She closed her eyes and pushed with her feet again to fly and feel the wind in her face. She knew He stood watching her, shining on her like the sun. After a while, the love inside her grew too large to bear, and she opened her mouth and let it overflow in a song.

Flying free, free as the eagle flies.
No chains to hold me down, no fear to hide the light.
Flying free, destination: sky.
Living free, free as the breeze that blows.

Growing free, free as the grass that grows.
Soaring free, drifting through the stars.

I smell the freedom in the air,
I see the life surrounding me.
I hear nature itself singing its song of freedom and life.
And I add my voice to the chorus, the chorus singing to You.
You are the One, the Giver of all life.
You are the One who gives us breath,
And You are our reason to sing!
For it was You that brought us from death. *

When she had finished, there were tears on both their faces, and she stopped the swing again. She scooted over. He came and sat beside her, and together they flew in the morning sun.

* *"Flying Free," copyright © 2000, by Sally Christopher.*

CHAPTER 7

Climate Considerations—3: A Breath of Fresh Air

One of the most beautiful images in the Bible is the picture of God bending over His new child and breathing into him the breath of life (see Genesis 2:7). That's so easy to say—"breath of life." But what in heaven's name is it? Nobody on the planet, not the most brilliant scientist or the greatest genius has one iota of an idea what life is. I'm not sure that those on other planets know much more, either! There, at least, they know its source and praise Creator God for the miracle that is solely His and, perhaps, more intrinsically Godlike than any other.

Life! It has a lot of names—nature, self, personality, mind, being, soul, spirit—each more mysterious than the previous one. That last one—spirit—is especially intriguing. In the original languages of the Bible, just as in English, the same word is used for the spirit of humanity and the Spirit of God. In Hebrew, the word is *ruach,* in Greek, *pneuma.* Interestingly, both these words are intrinsically linked with wind or air, and therefore with the breath of life. Yet we always understand spirit to be much more than merely the breath in our lungs. When we speak of our spirit, we mean *who we are.* Jesus called the Holy Spirit "He." He spoke of One who would come and teach and convict and lead (see John chapters 14–17). Paul and Isaiah both spoke of One who could be grieved (see Ephesians 4:30; Isaiah 63:10). You could say that the Holy Spirit does in the whole world what Jesus did in a small part of it for a few years—He manifests to us *who God is.*

But He's invisible, and He remains a mystery, this Spirit of God who knows us, but whom we cannot really know (see John 14:26; 15:26; 16:13, 14). During His late-night discussion with Nicodemus (see John 3), Jesus made the connection between the Spirit and wind more graphically than anyone else in the Bible. Read the whole conversation and especially note verse 8: " 'The wind blows where it wishes and you hear the sound of it, but do not know where it comes from and where it is going; so is everyone who is born of the Spirit.' " So it is not only the Spirit Himself who is mysterious—His children are too. When we receive Him, we join in that great mystery of the ages and become partakers of the divine nature (see 1 Peter 1:4).

Watch it happen on the Day of Pentecost, A.D. 31. The upper room must have been a large one, because there were 120 men and women gathered there (see Acts 1:15). They had been meeting together, praying, studying, and talking about the unbelievable things that had happened before their eyes in the preceding few weeks. Then the holy day came, and suddenly the room was filled with a rushing, roaring sound. It was a tornado; it was a tempest; it was the breath of life! Along with the wind came the fire and the tongues and more power than any of them had dreamed, even though Jesus had promised them that power would come upon them from on high (see Acts 1:8). Life was never the same for any of them. Life was never the same for any of *us.*

Our prayers change. From inside, "the Spirit . . . helps our weakness; for we do not know how to pray as we should, but the Spirit Himself intercedes for us with groanings too deep for words; and He who searches the hearts knows what the mind of the Spirit is, because He intercedes for the saints according to the will of God" (Romans 8:26, 27). Our lives change. We are transformed by His indwelling presence. Surviving and acquiring and doing—things that used to seem so important—fade away, and new things—love, joy, peace, *being*—become vital to us.

Then, as we live and move and have our being from within this new, fresher, clearer air, the breath of the soul becomes prayer. Just as your breathing changes to fit your needs, just as there are different kinds of wind, from a gentle breeze to a mighty tempest, so there are different kinds of prayer. Every one of them is as necessary to the soul's garden as physical air is to the trees and flowers.

Possibly most important is the discipline of what we might call "daily breathing exercises." This is your daily devotional time. Without it, you will do no work at all in your devotional life, and your garden will languish. Every Christian needs fixed times of prayer on a daily basis. There is the first-thing-in-the-morning "Good Morning, Lord" prayer time. This tunes your heart for the day and arms you against whatever might be ahead. Then there are mealtimes. "Saying grace" can easily become a meaningless habit, but it won't if you pray attentively. Think about what you're saying. Think about what is on your table, and what is *not* on millions of other tables in the world. Some of you reading this book know what it means to be hungry. If you don't, you might benefit from going without a meal or two now and then, just to remind yourself. And before bed, don't forget the "Goodnight, Lord, and Thank You for Your Companionship" prayer time. Those are the minimum. Daniel felt he needed prayer three times a day (see Daniel 6:10), and that probably didn't include his thanks for his food. Psalm 119:164 says, "Seven times a day I praise Thee."

At least one of your prayer times—morning or evening or whenever your personality warrants it—should include serious intercessory prayer for yourself and others. Some people keep detailed prayer lists; others are more spontaneous. The Holy Spirit has given to some the special gift of intercessory prayer, so that it becomes their work for God. They are His Prayer Warriors, exceedingly necessary to His work in the world. Whatever your personal style, this prayer time *must* include both talking and listening. We are pretty rude to God most of the time. We wouldn't think of talking to someone else the way we talk to Him, and then walking away without even giving that person a chance to get a word in edgewise. *Amen* doesn't mean "over and out."

The second kind of prayer is "continual prayer." If we were to practice deep-breathing exercises morning, noon, and night, the goal would be to make our breathing deeper and healthier all day long. So it is with prayer. As we grow in the habit of turning to God, we will do so more and more until our faces follow Him across the sky of our lives as sunflowers follow the sun from east to west. This prayer is sometimes conscious and worded, but often is just an attitude of knowing the Gardener is nearby. A smile, a sigh, or a tear can be a wordless prayer.

The Bible contains many, many passages concerning constant prayer. You will find some at the end of this chapter. Here is one of my favorites: "The Lord is near. Be anxious for nothing, but in everything by prayer and supplication with thanksgiving let your requests be made known to God. And the peace of God, which surpasses all comprehension, shall guard your hearts and your minds in Christ Jesus" (Philippians 4:5-7). Verse 7, in my opinion, reads even better from the Amplified Bible: "And God's peace [be yours, that tranquil state of a soul assured of its salvation through Christ, and so fearing nothing from God and being content with its earthly lot of whatever sort that is, that peace] which transcends all understanding, shall garrison *and* mount guard over your hearts and minds in Christ Jesus."* Did you notice? That ruby-encrusted watchtower the Gardener is building around your heart is partly built of prayer! You can help Him to keep you safe. That's why Jesus begged the disciples in the Garden of Gethsemane to pray—so that they would not enter into temptation. I wonder how the story would have been different if they had.

The Bible uses incense as the image of these prayers rising continually before the throne of God. In the tabernacle, that is what the altar of incense represented, standing before the veil separating it from the ark of the covenant. God told Moses that there should " 'be perpetual incense before the Lord throughout your generations' " (Exodus 30:8). When Jesus died, the veil was torn from top to bottom, and now we may enter "within the veil" (Hebrews 6:19) and "draw near with confidence to the throne of grace, that we may receive mercy and may find grace to help in time of need" (Hebrews 4:16). David prayed, "May my prayer be counted as incense before Thee; the lifting up of my hands as the evening offering" (Psalm 141:2). In Revelation 5:8 and 8:3, 4, there are golden bowls of incense which are the "prayers of all the saints."

Think what a relief it must be to God to breathe in the "sweet savor" of the prayers of His children, soaring above the death and destruction, the anger and despair that rise from His beloved little planet in a darkening stench. Add to that the fact that prayer gives God the right to work in the lives of those who would never pray for themselves, and you begin to see why God spends so much time and Bible print on the importance of prayer. It's almost the only way you can ever do any work in someone else's garden. And it's the only way your own will ever grow.

The third kind of prayer is "corporate prayer." Jesus said, " 'Again I say to you, that if two of you agree on earth about anything that they may ask, it shall be done for them by My Father who is in heaven. For where two or three have gathered together in My name, there I am in their midst' " (Matthew 18:19, 20). That's pretty sweeping! It's clear that if Jesus is in our midst, then we will do our best to ask according to His will and be relieved to remember that the Spirit translates our prayers for us, phrasing them in the way they really should be voiced and harmonizing them with the will of God. But it's also clear that God has chosen to give power to group prayer.

The disciples were praying "in one accord" in the upper room. Several times Paul asks the believers to pray with and for him. And there are several stories in both the Old and New Testaments that show group prayer at work. One is the story of Esther.

Imagine how frightening the situation was for Esther. The king, her husband, didn't even know she was a Jew. Now, at the instigation of Haman, he had decreed that all Jews, young and old, men, women, and children must be destroyed.

Mordecai sent word to Esther: "Can't you do something? He'll listen to you!"

But Esther sent back the reply, "If I go in without being summoned, I'll be killed, unless he's in a good mood and holds out his scepter. And he hasn't called me to him for a whole month! What chance do I have that he'll be glad to see me?"

Mordecai's reply has become classic. "Don't think you'll be safe in the king's palace. If you don't do something, God will use some other instrument, and maybe you'll die anyway. And who knows whether God didn't send you into the king's court just for such a time as this?"

So Esther took a deep breath and made her request. "Get all the Jews in Susa together, and fast and pray for three days with me. Then I'll go, and if I die, we're all going to die anyway."

Esther and her maids were closed away in the house of the women. She couldn't see even Mordecai, let alone anyone else. Yet she felt the power of all her people praying with her. And when she went before the king, God went before her. He could have saved His people some other way. But He asked a woman to help Him. And she said Yes.

What constitutes corporate prayer in your life? Obviously, this includes church attendance and prayer. Do you have family worship too? Do you have a prayer partner or a prayer group? Or both? Have you ever tried fasting and prayer together?

I once was strongly impressed to begin a fast. I had no idea why. Bewildered, I said, "OK, Lord. How long?"

I didn't seem to hear an answer, so I began a water-only fast. I prayed for whatever it was God wanted to accomplish. A day passed. Two days. On the third day I began to feel strong hunger. I felt the fast was over, and I still didn't know why I had been asked to do it. That day someone special to me, someone I had prayed about for years, told me he had given his heart to God.

I don't claim to understand fasting. It may clear the mind and help it to focus on God. It certainly purifies and cleanses the body, which of course includes the brain. But there's obviously more at work than physical things. God has given power to fasting and prayer.

There is one other specific kind of prayer that cannot be too highly stressed; it's the one kind of prayer we tend to practice the least. I'm talking about praise and adoration. It's pretty easy to pray prayers of praise when things are going beautifully and life seems almost perfect. Or is it? Do we wake up in the morning singing songs of thanksgiving to God for the endless blessings He showers on us? For years, my life was so painful that now I think it's almost heaven because it doesn't hurt anymore. But I'm not sure just the contrast alone would have taught me to praise God. I've seen people, miserable in terrible lives, still miserable when their circumstances change and their lives are easier. I reluctantly suspect I praise God now only because He taught me to sing in the dark.

In my youth I heard Steve Marshall preach on James 1:2-4. "Consider it all joy, my brethren, when you encounter various trials, knowing that the testing of your faith produces endurance. And let endurance have its perfect result, that you may be perfect and complete, lacking in nothing." In his inimitable way, Steve joked and demonstrated for us, dancing with joy when a trial comes. We laughed, but I knew he meant it, or rather, I knew the Bible meant it. It sounded good—I certainly liked the last part—but it sounded hard!

I've heard lots of other preachers say it too. "Praise God *in* the trouble!" "The God of the mountain is still God in the valley!" You've heard them, too, haven't you? It's easy to say. It's even easy to agree with. In church. But you have to make a choice.

So I started practicing. Beside an incubator, where a respirator breathed for my tiny son, I whispered, "Weeping may last for the night, but a shout of joy comes in the morning" "Hear, O Lord, and be gracious to me; O Lord, be Thou my helper' " (Psalm 30:5, 10). And two weeks later I wrote in my journal, "Thou hast turned for me my mourning into dancing; Thou hast loosed my sackcloth and girded me with gladness; that my soul may sing praises to Thee, and not be silent. O Lord my God, I will give thanks to Thee forever" (Psalm 30:11, 12).

Years later, racing through the night to the emergency room with the same beloved son, I comforted him and myself by singing every praise song I knew. My voice wavered, choked with tears and fright, but the Spirit prayed for us both—and again a miracle followed.

The miracle doesn't always follow. Or rather, it isn't always the one you wanted. The miracle can be only on the inside of you. Facing divorce, I sang tearful Scripture songs. "My heart is steadfast, O Lord, my heart is steadfast, I will sing. Awake my spirit, awake my spirit. I will awake at dawn of day."

And long nights of asthma attacks have given a whole new meaning to Psalm 150:6: "Let everything that has breath praise the Lord"!

Over the years, I've learned a lot of things about praise. I learned that it doesn't have to feel true. It can even feel like an outright lie. (My heart is *not* steadfast; it's falling apart in a million pieces!!) You are stating your faith that God is truly in control. And no matter how your emergency turns out, it's true that He really knows what He's doing. He is in control of the circumstances. The question is: Is He in control of your heart? That part is up to you.

Believe me, if your garden is in a shambles as you read this, if you cry yourself to sleep at night, if you have secrets you can't talk about even to God, let alone anyone else, I know how hard this is to swallow. I *know*. But I promise you on my life, it is true. Praise is exercise. It's hard. It makes you sweaty. It gets you out of breath. Sometimes it hurts. But it makes you strong. Because " 'the joy of the Lord is your strength' " (Nehemiah 8:10). And like Jesus, I believe we will see the fruits of the anguish and travail of our souls and be satisfied (see Isaiah 53:11)—especially when we compare our anguish with His!

"Beloved, do not be surprised at the fiery ordeal among you, which comes upon you for your testing, as though some strange thing were happening to you; but to the degree that you share the sufferings of Christ, keep on rejoicing; so that also at the revelation of His glory, you may rejoice with exultation" (1 Peter 4:12, 13).

Amen! *Praise the Lord!*

---

*(In the Amplified Bible, brackets indicate an addition or amplification by the translator; italicized "and" means that the original word contains both English concepts.)

DIG DEEPER

Since Jesus now has a human body and is connected to the human race in a way He never was before, His presence is with us now through the Holy Spirit. Jesus seems to tell us (see John chapters 14–17) that after He goes to His Father, the Holy Spirit will be to us what Jesus was to His disciples while He was on earth—only more so. What does this mean to you? How is the Holy Spirit "Jesus" to you in your daily life?

How have your prayers and your life changed since the Holy Spirit broke through into your life? How has He made it possible for you to speak to people in "their" language in a way you could not have done before?

When and how do you do your "daily breathing exercises"?

When and how do you do serious intercessory prayer?

Is the attitude of continual prayer growing into your life as deeply as you would like? Here is a list of some of the passages in the Bible on continual prayer. You may study and meditate on them for further inspiration. Acts 12:5; Romans 12:12; Ephesians 6:18; Colossians 4:2; 1 Peter 4:7; 1 Timothy 2:5; 1 Thessalonians 3:10.

What does it mean to you personally that we can now enter into the Most Holy Place behind the torn veil, and "come boldly before the throne of grace"?

How and when do you take part in corporate, or group, prayer? Ask God if there are ways He'd like to enlarge this part of your spiritual life.

Have you ever fasted and prayed? If so, write or think about a time when this brought blessing to your life. If not, study into the subject and ask God if there are times He would like you to make fasting a part of your prayer life.

How much is praise and adoration a part of your daily life? We can never praise God enough. In your journal, write a hymn of praise and love to Him, remembering that praise and adoration are about *who God is*, as opposed to thanksgiving, which is thanks for *what God does*. If you need inspiration, take a psalm of praise and personalize it to be meaningful to God and you alone.

Snapshots From My Garden

The watchtower was finished! She couldn't take her eyes off its shining beauty and perfect symmetry. The sun shone and sparkled from its rubies and sapphires and its crystal windows. She turned in a circle, taking in all that had changed so far. The low wall, which now felt so safe and comforting, was a work of art in itself. The Tree stood in the center, spreading its wide branches clustered with leaves bigger and greener than they had ever been. The spring at its roots bubbled into the little stone-lined pool and overflowed through the channel under the wall. The rubble and trash had been cleared away so the whole area seemed much larger than before.

The garden looked wonderful! And . . . bare. Aside from the Tree, the only green things were her few plants from before, tucked away in their shady corner. They had been so weak and straggly. Some had been taken away by the Gardener. When she had asked, He had told her she didn't need those plants. The ones He had left her were beginning to grow stronger and greener. But they were so few. The ground looked barren.

She turned again, and the Gardener was there. He had a large roll of paper in His hand. "Look," He invited, and spread out the roll on the ground. She came and sat beside Him, trying to make sense of the lines and figures on the paper.

"It is time to begin preparing the ground for planting," He told her.

She looked up from the paper and around at the garden again—and felt some dismay. It was so big! There was a lot to do already; how much more was He going to ask of her?

The Gardener's hand brought her face back to look at Him. "Stay with Me," He said, smiling. "I said it is time to begin. We don't need to do everything at once." He pointed to the paper. "Here is where we will start. At first, the two most important places in the garden are the center garden, around your tree, and the door garden, where people will look in when they come to visit. We want our garden to be nurturing to you and welcoming to all. First we'll dig up the ground around the tree and the spring. We will probably have to bring in soil, too, because we don't want to harm the tree's roots." He glanced up at the tree. "It could use some feeding, anyway."

She followed His gaze. The Tree needed feeding? How do you feed a tree? And how did He know? It looked beautiful to her—more beautiful than it had in all her life! He was speaking again, and she brought her attention back to His hand pointing and moving on the paper. "We'll dig and plow around the gate too. What do you think of an arbor there, with vines trained over it?"

What did she think? He was asking her? "It's Your garden, remember? You bought it," she said. "Anyway, You're the expert."

"It's our garden. There will be many choices you can make."

She looked at the gate. A picture took shape in her mind. It felt rather daring. Breathlessly, she said, "I think an arbor would be wonderful!"

He watched her. "And?"

"Well . . ." she looked into His encouraging eyes. "What if . . . could we build it wide, so there would be room under it in the shade, for benches? In case we have visitors."

His wide smile made her feel warm all over. "Terrific idea!" He said. "I am so happy to see you begin to welcome the idea of visitors, instead of fearing them. Some of them have been just as hurt and afraid as you; they can learn from you—and you from them."

He rolled up His plans and stood. "Well, then, let's get to work. There are shovels, forks, and hoes in the corner over there. I'll show you how to use them."

It was backbreaking, frustrating, slow, tedious work. They accumulated a wheelbarrow full of stones, dead stumps, and old weeds. She also accumulated blisters, bruises, and muscle aches. But little by little, the ground around the Tree grew soft and dark and rich smelling. At the end of the day, she felt exhausted.

Cleaned up, the tools put away for the night, they sat in the swing together, moved gently by the Gardener's foot. She felt herself smiling, and realized that under the exhaustion, there was exhilaration. "Tomorrow," she whispered.

Tomorrow, the blisters would become calluses, and she would become strong. And her garden would be beautiful.

She felt a chuckle beside her. "Maybe the day after tomorrow," He said.

CHAPTER 8

Site Preparation: Who's Wearing the Harness?

There is a funny thing about gardens. The weeds grow and flourish vibrantly with no effort on anyone's part, but if you want flowers, fruit, vegetables—anything useful, in fact—then you have to do all kinds of work. It's true in our souls, too, have you noticed? It must have something to do with a broken and sinful world because, in truth, God never created a weed. And many of the plants we think of as weeds, because they've become such pests here, were meant to be not only useful, but health-giving. Believe it or not, that can be true of our souls, as well, once the Master Gardener moves in. But that's a subject for another chapter. Right now, we're plowing and disking and harrowing and tilling. Nowadays we do these things with machines, but that's only so we can do more, not to make it really *easier*. I just did it yesterday, and I'm still sore!

So, even though weeds don't seem to need soft, loose, rich, aerated loam (they just grow happily in regular old dirt), the plants we want to grow are more picky. Not only are they more picky as a class, they each have their own individual ideas of the conditions they want. Is that true of virtues such as faith, hope, and patience, too? Are there different conditions that will encourage the growth of different values? What exactly does it mean to plow or till a soul, anyway?

Well, have you ever heard of a "harrowing experience"? Yes, that expression came directly from agricultural life. A harrow, for those who don't know, is a large attachment that tractors or horses can pull over plowed ground. It can have rows of long iron teeth to break up the soil or it can have discs set at an angle to slice into the ground from different directions. So *harrowing* is used now to mean an experience that tears you up emotionally, physically, mentally, or spiritually, or sometimes all of the above.

Speakers or singers often use the imagery of plowing or harrowing to represent trials or tribulations that come to us and the way God can use these to develop our characters. I think that's true. But I found an interesting twist in Hosea 10. Early in this chapter, God has been very harsh with Israel because "he produces fruit for himself ... [but his] heart is faithless" (verses 1, 2). In other words, Israel has said No to the Master Gardener and prefers to do it himself. So God says, "Ephraim is a trained heifer that loves to thresh, [threshing is more fun, because it comes after the harvest, and includes parties and celebration] but I will come over her fair neck with a yoke; I will harness Ephraim, Judah will plow, Jacob will harrow for himself" (verse 11).

You mean I can do some of the work? How can that be? Let's look at the next verse: "Sow with a view to righteousness, reap in accordance with kindness; break up your fallow ground, for it is time to seek the Lord until He comes to rain righteousness on you" (verse 12). Wow! But when I've tried to work before, it's been a disaster! Verse 13: "You have plowed wickedness, you have reaped injustice, you have eaten the fruit of lies. *Because you have trusted in your way*" (emphasis supplied).

Truthfully, I must admit that ever since I learned the glorious truth about salvation by grace alone, I've had trouble understanding my part of the work. I used to think I did it all myself—"with God's help," of course. Then I thought He saved me by Himself, but I behaved out of gratitude—a wonderful idea with only one flaw. It doesn't work. Some people talk of wearing a yoke with Jesus, but that still makes us equal partners, and I'm uncomfortable with that. Then I learned that God really does all the work Himself—"both to will and to work for His good pleasure" (Philippians 2:13). But He uses my hands to do the work, and I still couldn't understand. I always either got caught up in trying to *do* perfectly, or sat around waiting for *Him* to do. I think the picture we're about to examine helps me understand more than any other.

It may be important to remember that the agricultural imagery in the Bible has no recourse to modern machinery. A farmer today gets in the tractor and steers it absolutely anywhere he wants it to go. I've kind of had that idea about grace, too—that I'm just a tool in His hands. Well, there is truth in that, but I am very unlike a tractor. I have a mind and will of my own, made and given me by God, and I think if He wanted robots, He'd have made them. And saved Himself infinite trouble, I might add!

Let's look, instead, at how plowing was done in Hosea's and Jesus' times. I live in an area where I can see these things on a daily basis. My part of the country is home to the largest concentration of Amish and Mennonite people in the United States. Thousands of them still use horses and buggies as their means of transportation and farm entirely with animal power. (This is probably still true in most parts of the world, by the way, but we tend to forget it in our modern, technology-laden countries.) Here is how it works.

The farmer leads the horse out of her stall or field. She can fight and put up a fuss, toss her head when he tries to put the bit in her mouth, or she can be gentle and calm. And since I have horses myself, I can tell you that what she does will depend on her relationship with her handler more than it will on her training, her experience, or anything else. Mind you, she'll still have moods and whims! But once she's learned from many, many past experiences that her handler can control her without hurting her, and that he will stay calm and patient no matter what she does, she will be calm and patient, too. That kind of relationship can take a long time to develop, but the Farmer under discussion never gets tired or loses His temper.

Next, our horse is led to the plow and hitched to it. Actually, most plowing is done with two or more horses—up to five if the field to be plowed is a new one. That would be an interesting image of people working together for and with God. But in this case, the imagery is of ourselves, plowing in our own garden, and one horse can do that. The farmer walks behind the plow, holding its handles to direct it, with the horse's reins looped around his neck so he can direct her. But the truth is, she'll be directed more by his voice commands.

Now, tell me this. Who's working? Who's in charge? What factors decide if the furrows will be smooth and even, or wildly divergent? Who decides where the plowing will be done, which direction the furrows should run, whether they should be straight or contoured, how long to work, and when to quit?

Here is my answer—it depends! A draft horse used for farm work can weigh up to a ton. The man may weigh 200 pounds. And while God is a lot bigger than we are, He has chosen to give us free will, and we can mess things up just as royally as any half-broken horse! I've done it.

A lot sometimes depends, too, on what the horse thinks *should* be done. This is most often a problem only in the best-trained horses. I once visited an Amish man to look at a horse he had for sale. When I arrived, he was plowing with a young horse harnessed between two older ones—another fruitful subject for consideration. He stopped plowing, left the plow in the field, since he would be going back out later, and brought the horses in.

Well, Queen, the old mare, knew perfectly well the plowing was not done. She also knew it wasn't lunchtime yet. While her master's hand was on the bridle, she came in obediently enough, but as soon as he let go of her inside the barn, she turned and went calmly and determinedly back out, with the farmer coming behind her, saying, "Queen! Queen! Whoa!" He caught her and brought her back, and again, she obeyed, but she clearly thought he was the one who was confused.

Have you ever secretly thought that God must be confused? Have you ever demanded that He explain why He was doing things out of their proper order—differently from the way He's told you to do them before? Have you tried to tell Him the way you were sure He *should* be working?

It seems to me that this grace-works conundrum can go wrong in two different ways. You can stand in the barn and expect God to do the plowing alone. Or you can try to do it yourself or your own way.

What is plowing or harrowing, anyway, as applied to our soul's gardens? Suppose we use the word *cultivate* instead. This is another word that has crept into daily use from the vocabulary of farmers. And since it is in daily use, we all know what we mean by it. My dictionary says, "to improve by care, training, or study; refine [to cultivate one's mind]; to promote the development or growth of; acquire and develop [to cultivate a taste for music]; to seek to develop familiarity with; give one's attention to; pursue."

In the last three chapters, we have begun to study some ways we can develop the discipline of working with God. As He sends His sunshine, rain, and fresh air, we practice spending time every day in His presence, breathing in prayer, and rejoicing in His rain even when it seems like a storm.

These things have begun our training so that now we can have a more concrete job. We can bend every effort of mind, soul, and body to improve our ability to receive and grow whatever seed He wants to plant in us. We don't even know what it is yet. But we can study, train, and refine our minds and our natures to get ready for it. We can develop familiarity with Him through His Word, and pursue and give our attention to everything He shows us. This doesn't just mean the part of life that we label spirituality, as in church and Bible study. It means that everything about our lives is new and exciting—our talents, our work, our families, the physical world. God teaches us through all these things. It takes time and effort to re-educate ourselves to think His way. Like the horse, we have to constantly learn, by many, many repeated experiences, to listen for the "word behind [us]" (Isaiah 30:21) telling us which way to go, how fast, and when and where to stop.

What if we rebel and refuse to work with God? Then He will do the work Himself, in a last desperate attempt to redeem our desolate waste-lands. Plowing can be punishment. "Zion will be plowed as a field, Jerusalem will become a heap of ruins, and the mountain of the temple will become high places of a forest" (Micah 3:12, cf. Jeremiah 26:18, 19). Why? Is it because God is really mad, and you've had it now? In the very next verse we find His heart's purpose: "And it will come about in the last days that the mountain of the house of the Lord will be estab-lished as the chief of the mountains. It will be raised above the hills, and the peoples will stream to it" (Micah 4:1).

That's the plan. But every individual has to choose. God has never and will never force anyone's will to bend to His—not for salvation, that is. Even the devils will eventually bow and confess His justice, whether they want to or not. But if you and I want the renewal to happen in our own souls, if we don't want to be on the outside looking into the garden of God's delights, *we must choose.*

And sometimes God is reduced to drastic measures. King Nebuchadnezzar's story provides a dramatic example.

At first, Nebuchadnezzar seems like a purely Bad Guy. He has taken over the whole world, or so it seems. Now he's after God's land. All the prophets say calmly, "Don't worry, God will never let anything bad hap-pen to His people."

Well, not *all* the prophets. There were some faithful ones, most no-tably Jeremiah. He insisted that God's protection was conditional and that if the people did not turn and repent, they would certainly be overrun. He said specifically that it would be Babylon who would do the overrunning, and that the captivity would last seventy years. He even said that God had chosen the instrument for the punishment of His people. So in Daniel 1:1, 2, we have Nebuchadnezzar besieging Jerusalem and the *Lord giving* into his pagan hands not only the city and the king and a lot of highborn youth, but even the vessels of the temple!

This looks like the story of Israel and Judah. And it is. And it's the story of Daniel. But God can keep billions of stories going at once and not get mixed up. Let's look closely at the story of Nebuchadnezzar himself.

He's a Bad Guy. A pagan king with a god complex, who has just destroyed the temple of the most holy God, thus proving to his own satisfaction that he is bigger. That's Act One.

Act Two: He has a dream he can't remember clearly or understand, and being a Bad Guy, he threatens to kill all his counselors unless someone not only can interpret it, but tell him what the dream was in the first place. Daniel and his friends pray as if their lives depend on it, and Daniel tells Nebuchadnezzar the dream and explains it.

Nebuchadnezzar likes the first part. " 'You, O king, are the king of kings, to whom the God of heaven has given the kingdom, the power, the strength, and the glory; and wherever the sons of men dwell, or the beasts of the field, or the birds of the sky, He has given them into your hand and has caused you to rule over them all. You are the head of gold' " (Daniel 2:37, 38).

Nebuchadnezzar's reaction to this, believe it or not, is to fall on his face, do homage to Daniel, and actually give offerings and incense to him, saying, " 'Surely your God is a God of gods and a Lord of kings and a revealer of mysteries, since you have been able to reveal this mystery' " (Daniel 2:46, 47). Instead of thinking he is bigger than God, Nebuchadnezzar has decided that God is pretty high even among the other gods, and that Daniel must be, too.

Act Three: On second thought, the more he ponders the matter, the less Nebuchadnezzar likes the idea that this "God of heaven" has *given* him all he has. And He especially doesn't care for the prophecy of other kingdoms after his. If he's the "king of kings," then his kingdom ought to last forever. He decides to make an image of his own. It'll be just like the one in his dream, except for one small detail—it will be *all* gold. Nebuchadnezzar will assemble everybody who's anybody and make them all bow down and worship him. The image, that is. One gets the distinct impression they are the same thing.

Daniel must be out of town, but his three friends are still there, and of course they do not bow down to Nebuchadnezzar, his decrees, or his image. They even have the nerve to say, "No, thanks, sir. We don't need a second chance. Our God can deliver us from the fire, and will in any case deliver us from *you*. We will not bow down to anyone but Him."

This time Nebuchadnezzar sees the Son of God with his own eyes. After he calls the other three, unburned, out of the fire, he proclaims, " 'Blessed be the God of Shadrach, Meshach and Abed-nego, who has sent His angel and delivered His servants who put their trust in Him, violating the king's command, and yielded up their bodies so as not to serve or worship any god except their own God. Therefore, I make a decree that any people, nation or tongue that speaks anything offensive against the God of Shadrach, Meshach and Abed-nego shall be torn limb from limb and their houses reduced to a rubbish heap, inasmuch as there is no other god who is able to deliver in this way' " (Daniel 3:28, 29). Now, God is the top God, and everyone has to respect Him or else! Luckily for Nebuchadnezzar, God doesn't feel that way, or Nebuchadnezzar would have been torn limb from limb, etc., in the next chapter!

Act Four: This act is found in Daniel chapter four. If you haven't read it, or even if you haven't read it recently, I strongly urge you to do so. As far as I know, this chapter is the only chapter of the Bible written by a pagan king, and by the end of the chapter, he is not a pagan anymore. The story is incredible. Here, God begins His serious gardening work.

Once again, King Nebuchadnezzar has a dream. He remembers this one, but it alarms him greatly. He calls all his magicians, and even though he tells them the dream, they can't tell him the meaning. So he calls Daniel, in whom by now Nebuchadnezzar recognizes " 'a spirit of the holy gods' " (Daniel 4:8).

"Here is the dream," he says. "I saw a great tree that filled the earth and provided food and shelter to every bird and animal. Then an angel came from heaven and ordered that the tree be chopped down, but the stump bound with brass and iron to keep it alive. The angel said, 'Let him live in the field as an animal for seven years, until he learns that it is

God who rules, and gives authority to whomever He wishes.' What does this dream mean?" (see verses 10-17).

It seems to me that almost anyone would be able to hazard a guess as to the meaning of this dream. Probably the magicians know, but are afraid to say it. Probably Nebuchadnezzar himself has a suspicion, or he wouldn't be so alarmed. Even Daniel is "appalled" and has a hard time answering.

"Oh, king," he says at last, "if only this dream was about your enemies! It means you will lose the power and glory you have now and live as a beast of the fields for seven years, until you learn that God is in charge, and gives the kingdoms of the earth to whomever He wishes. So please, your majesty, change your ways now, do righteousness, and show mercy to the poor, and maybe it will at least be put off!" (see verses 19-27).

The king either tries to follow his advice or God is very patient, because another whole year passes. Then one day Nebuchadnezzar is on his rooftop—probably in those famed hanging gardens. He looks around on his marble city and murmurs to himself, " ' "Is this not Babylon the great, which I myself have built as a royal residence by the might of my power and for the glory of my majesty?" ' " (verse 30).

Nebuchadnezzar is a lucky man. Or rather, a blessed man. God doesn't always teach someone so directly. " 'While the word was in the king's mouth, a voice came from heaven, saying, "King Nebuchadnezzar, to you it is declared: sovereignty has been removed from you, and you will be driven away from mankind, and your dwelling place will be with the beasts of the field. You will be given grass to eat like cattle, and seven periods of time [years] will pass over you, until you recognize that the Most High is ruler over the realm of mankind, and bestows it on whomever He wishes" ' " (verses 31, 32).

And so it begins. Perhaps it is Daniel who holds the kingdom together until the seven long years pass. It is certainly unheard of in those violent times for a king to still have a kingdom after being away seven years, let alone after seven years of insanity! At the end of the seven years, Nebuchadnezzar, shaggy-haired and clawed like a bird, with no vestige of a kingly robe, looks up to heaven. This is a very telling phrase. He looks up. His reason returns—or maybe for the first time, true reason comes to him—and he praises God! What a miracle! He goes back to court, his nobles begin to "seek him out," and more glory than ever is given to him. But now he knows where that glory comes from. Here is the conclusion of his letter:

" 'Now I Nebuchadnezzar praise, exalt, and honor the King of heaven, for all His works are true and His ways just, and He is able to humble those who walk in pride' " (verse 37).

To me, this is one of the best stories in the whole Bible. It makes me redouble my prayers for those I know who seem as if they're so caught up in their own ways and ideas that they will never turn to God. And it soothes my fears that I myself will be blind to something God wants to teach me. Because if the King of heaven can convince King Nebuchadnezzar, He can convince anyone!

This story also teaches that even if a person rebels and has to undergo the kind of punishing plowing described Micah 3 and Jeremiah 26, there can still be renewal. No heart is so hard that God *cannot* soften it. The person has to decide to cooperate, that's all. Here is what God said to the nation with which He had to be so harsh: " ' "I have sworn that surely the nations which are around you [which God Himself had used in judgment on Israel] will themselves endure their insults. But . . . you will put forth your branches and bear your fruit. . . . For, behold, *I am for you*, and I will turn to you, and you shall be cultivated and sown. . . . Thus you will know that I am the Lord" ' " (Ezekiel 36:7-9, 11, emphasis supplied). Nebuchadnezzar made that choice, and learned to know who God is and that His only plan is for us to both plow and thresh in hope (see 1 Corinthians 9:10).

Most of all, this story makes me want to cooperate with the Master Gardener. He's done some drastic remodeling and rebuilding in my garden, but He's never actually cut down my tree! I never want to be so stubborn that He has to! I want to let him harness me and plow and till and cultivate as much as He needs to, trusting that He will do just what is needed, not a bit more nor a bit less.

Sometimes I have thought He doesn't know when to stop. But He does—really. Listen to Isaiah 28:24: "Does the farmer plow continually to plant seed? Does he continually turn and harrow the ground?" Later in the same chapter, using the imagery of threshing, Isaiah says, "He does not continue to thresh it forever. Because the wheel of his cart and his horses eventually damage it, he does not thresh it longer. This also comes from the Lord of hosts, who has made His counsel wonderful and His wisdom great" (verses 28, 29).

He knows just when to stop. He knows just how much preparation the soil of our hearts—yours and mine—need in order to grow the virtues He has planned. Then He'll start planting.

DIG DEEPER

Write or think about a harrowing experience you have had, for which you are grateful today, because of the fertility it brought to your spiritual life. If you have not dedicated your harrowing experiences, of whatever type, to God and let Him bless them, if you are drowning in bitterness and doubt, take those burdens immediately to God and let Him take them. No, it's not easy, but it can and must be done if you are to live and grow. God can do it. He promises.

Do some serious thinking or writing about how well you cooperate with God when He harnesses you to work for Him. How well-trained a "horse" are you? Are you an intelligent part of the process God is working out in your life? Do you listen intently for His voice behind you, telling you which way to go, how far, and when to stop?

List some specific ways that God is teaching you to cultivate your mind, soul, and body to grow strong and to work for Him. Ask Him if there are new directions He'd like you to take.

Has there ever been a time when you really rebelled and were disciplined by God in order to bring you back to a sense of yourself and of Him? If so, don't think too much about the rebellion—it's forgiven and buried. But remember the ways He led you back, and sing His praises!

Snapshots From My Garden

She stretched her aching back and groaned. The joints popped like twigs burning on a crackling fire. Come to think of it, parts of her felt like fire, too. She looked around. Dirt. Nothing but dirt. Heaps and hollows and furrows and plains of endless brown dirt! Plenty of tomorrows had come and gone, and they didn't seem to have made much progress.

The Gardener called, and she joined Him—more out of duty than desire.

"What's the matter, My child?"

She scuffed her toe in the dirt. She was sick of the stuff! She really ought not to complain . . .

"Well?" He asked gently.

She knew by now that He could read her every mood, anyway. Finally, she burst out, "Is it ever going to look like anything?"

To her surprise, He laughed. She looked up, which was a mistake if she wanted to remain grumpy. She struggled against the impulse to smile back. "What's so funny?"

"Look around," said the Gardener.

She did. Sure enough—dirt.

"And think back," prompted the Gardener.

She hung her head and scuffed her toe again. "I know. You mean there's been progress. And I agree, and I don't mean to be impatient, or ungrateful . . ." Looking up, directly into His smiling eyes this time, she added earnestly, "I really don't! But I want a garden! A real, growing garden that people can see and enjoy and . . ." Her eyes fell again. "That You can be proud of."

His arm came around her. "I am proud of you now. You have done more than you know and have tried hard to cooperate with everything I've asked of you, even when you didn't understand, and even when it hurt or frightened you. I am proud of you! Anyway, it so happens I have a surprise for you today. Look here."

She looked. He held open the tool pouch at His waist, and she saw bright packets, many of them. A rising breeze of excitement blew away the last of her crossness. "Seeds? Today? Are we going to plant them today?"

He laughed again at her eagerness. "Today. And better yet, since you're so impatient for results . . ."

She followed His pointing hand. "Flowers!" she cried, dropping to her knees beside the flat of bright little faces.

"I have grown some transplants for you. See, here are the vines of Friendship that will grow over our arbor and some bright Welcome flowers for our door garden. And these are ferns and Peace flowers that love shade, for our own special place under the Tree."

She turned and threw her arms around Him, hiding her face in His shoulder. "I'm sorry," she whispered. "Again." It seemed she was always sorry for something.

"Never mind," He whispered back. "You need to discard the crossness, but never apologize for longing for growth in your garden. It's what I want, too, much more than you realize. It's happening, whether you see it or not. And remember—I am proud of you just as you are."

CHAPTER 9

Planting: The Spirit Went Out to Sow

"He presented another parable to them, saying, 'The kingdom of heaven is like a mustard seed, which a man took and sowed in his field; and this is smaller than all other seeds; but when it is full grown, it is larger than the garden plants, and becomes a tree, so that the birds of the air come and nest in its branches' " (Matthew 13:31, 32).

There is more here than meets the eye. Who is the man? We usually look at this parable in conjunction with the other two references to mustard seeds—Matthew 17:20 and Luke 17:6. In these, Jesus defines the mustard seed as faith. "Even if you have only a mustard-seed's worth of faith, you can move mountains." We infer that the man is ourselves, and we are to plant and cultivate faith in our lives. True! But could the parable be given a different twist? In other "kingdom of heaven" parables, the "man" is usually God. If God is the Gardener, and we are His field, and *He* is the One who plants and grows the faith, the story takes on an entirely new life, at least in my mind. This is the point of view from which we are studying the gardening imagery of the Bible. God is the Gardener, and we are both the fertile ground (at least we're fertile once He digs in all the manure He finds necessary!) and the caretaker. So

God plants the faith. The more we work and cooperate with Him, the bigger that faith grows, but we must never forget that He is the One with the landscape plans, not to mention the only One with seeds.

In the last chapter, we theorized that virtues, like plants, require different kinds of preparation in the soil of our lives, and that only the Master Gardener knows how much of which preparation we need. We looked at Isaiah 28:24. "Does the farmer plow continually to plant seed? Does he continually turn and harrow the ground?" It might seem as if He does, but eventually He stops and starts planting. "Does he not level its surface, and sow dill and scatter cummin, and plant wheat in rows, barley in its place, and rye within its area?" (verse 25).

How could we apply this to the qualities, gifts, and virtues we long to see growing in our lives? Are some characteristics sown, some scattered, and some planted in rows? Does each virtue have its proper area? If we were to use our gardening imaginations, we might have vines trained over trellises, some flowers in neat beds, some naturalized under trees, and ground covers left to grow wild to cover a steep hillside. One important point to remember is that no garden can be planted all in one day. Like earthly gardeners, Jesus does each part of the landscaping in its own time, usually not in the order we would have dictated. He doesn't grow impatient, as we do, to have everything done and perfect *now.*

I know from experience that it is God who will decide where and how to plant and grow love, joy, peace, and all the rest. Take patience, for instance. It's the perfect example. When I ask God for patience, I want Him to magically make me stop *wanting* to get mad when things don't go my way. I don't want Him to make a million things suddenly not go my way, so that I can practice being patient anyway! But that's what He does, every time. When I ask for peace, I want freedom from strife, not lots of opportunities to grow a sense of peacefulness in His presence in the middle of strife! But He's the Gardener, and I have to believe He knows more about the work than I ever will. Let's look at some of the things God plants in us.

Galatians 5:22, 23 lists some of the basic fruits God considers indispensable in His gardens. These can be listed in various ways. Here's the way they appear in my Bible: love, joy, peace, patience, kindness, good-ness, faithfulness, gentleness, self-control. Let's look at some of the ways God plants these qualities in the hearts of His children.

First and most important, we must remember that these are fruits *of the Spirit.* Jesus says in John 15 that He is the Vine and we are the branches, and that we can grow nothing unless we are planted in Him. So let's repeat the obvious. These fruits are declared yours as soon as you accept Jesus and let Him bring His tools and move in. If you split open an apple seed and examine it minutely, you will find a minuscule stem, root, and embryonic leaves. The whole tree and all its future crops of hundreds, thousands, maybe millions of apples, are there in the seed. Not to mention all the trees those future apples could grow and the apples *those* trees could grow . . . Likewise, the newest of newborn Christians contains, with Jesus and His Spirit, all the fruits listed above in total perfection. Wow! Think about that for a minute!

So you could say that before the Gardener ever started breaking down and building, developing the spring, digging and manuring and culti-vating, the fruit was there, in *His* heart. But how, practically speaking, does He plant the individual virtues, once He really starts to plant?

LOVE

A very credible case can be made for the concept that love is the only fruit and that all the other things in the list are aspects of love. But in practical terms, we caretakers need all the specifics we can get, and I think it helps to study each quality independently.

So where does love begin? This seems obvious. Love comes from God. He loves us, so we love Him. And since we love Him, we begin to love ourselves and others. Obvious, but never neat and simple. Take a look at yesterday. Looking back, do you see yourself as loving those you meet just as Jesus does? Don't get discouraged; the tree has to grow before you see the visible fruit. Does love come easier now than it did before you first believed? That's where you see the growth. Still, I had been a Christian for many years when I prayed one day (for at least the millionth time), "Please, Lord, give me more love! Make me more loving!"

I was a young mother at the time, and the most important people in my world—my three babies—always got the sharpest side of my tongue. I would have died for them, but I couldn't seem to live for them. I was so discouraged. I saw myself standing before Jesus, head hanging, weeping, begging for more love to give my children.

"Please," I begged, over and over. I felt as if He wasn't answering me. Then something told me to look up. In my heart, I looked up at His face, and was startled to see Him with His arms outstretched.

"Well, come here," He said. And He held me close.

I have never forgotten that moment. It had never occurred to me to think of it in that light. I had meant, "Give me more love," in the sense of giving me *something*. As if He would open my brain and pour in some substance that would make me patient and kind. But I saw that the same sentence, "Give me more love," could be interpreted the way Jesus had interpreted it for me. By giving His love to me, wrapping His arms around me and pressing me to His heart, He would increase my store of love and make me more able to give it. It was such an eye-opener!

I still get frustrated at how long it's taking to grow to maturity. But I did get a chance to see this principle in visible action not long ago. A woman came to me and said sorrowfully that she desperately needed more love for her husband and son. I grinned and held out my arms. She stared, just as I had. I told her the story and held her and told her the hug was from God, and that there were plenty more where that one came from. You should have seen her face. That hug filled us both up!

And that's the way He works. You need more love? Go get some! He has plenty, and it's all for you.

If love were a plant, I think it would be ivy. It grows all over everything, chokes out weeds, covers unsightly messes, softens walls, never hurts anyone, and stays green all year. It thrives on care, but faithfully survives even when trampled and ignored, as long as the Gardener is still in residence. You can grow more by cutting off shoots and rooting them, and in fact, the more shoots you cut off and share, the thicker and more lush your ivy will be.

JOY

Joy is one of those tricky virtues to define. It's like happiness, but not exactly. Happiness comes from having things go the way you hoped they would. Joy has to be able to live even when everything's going wrong. " 'The joy of the Lord is your strength' " (Nehemiah 8:10). So if our strength depends on joy, then it has to be strong and indestructible, deep-rooted. That means it's not just your joy, not human joy, it's the joy *of the Lord*. It is in His presence that we find everlasting joy.

Like the rest of the fruits, joy first comes when Jesus comes in. "I will rejoice greatly in the Lord, my soul will exult in my God; for He has clothed me with garments of salvation, He has wrapped me with a robe of righteousness. . . . For as the earth brings forth its sprouts, and as a garden causes the things sown in it to spring up, so the Lord God will cause righteousness and praise to spring up before all the nations" (Isaiah 61:10, 11).

Have you ever been privileged to see the face of someone who has just at that moment truly believed? Or do you remember the way you felt when you first let the Gardener in? Suddenly you find out that the God of the universe loves you, died for you, and will *cause* righteousness to spring up in you, with no help from you! It's not something you have to do or be or get or learn or buy. It's His, and He's giving it to you. If you really understand this with all your heart, it will keep joy alive deep down inside on the very darkest days you can imagine. In the depths of pain and fear you can know that this will pass and that there is a whole heaven waiting for you. That's joy.

Happiness is very nice and should be in every garden. It has bright, sweet-smelling blossoms, like petunias. But it's just an annual. The blossoms fade, and the first frost does it in. Be sure you let God plant plenty of true, perennial joy. Joy is more like wild daisies. They come up all over the place where you least expect them, their blossoms last, they are impossible to kill, and even when they're not in bloom, they're still there, rooted, growing, and waiting.

PEACE

Jesus said He gives us peace, as He gives us all other blessings. But He also warns that His peace is not like the world's peace. The world (and I) would define peace as, tranquillity, calm absence of conflict. Jesus' definition is different. He says, " '*Let* not your heart be troubled, nor *let* it be fearful' " (John 14:27, emphasis supplied). That word *let* implies a choice on our part. We choose not to allow fear and worry to live in our garden. And then in the same breath as " 'in Me you may have peace,' " Jesus warns that, " 'in the world you have tribulation' " (John 16:33). Thanks a lot! I thought You said I could have peace! To Him, peace and tribulation are not mutually exclusive. " 'Take courage,' " He continues. Here is another action word. Take it. Pick it up. Plant it deep. Because (and here's another clue) " 'I *have* overcome the world' " (verse 33, emphasis supplied).

Now wait a minute. Jesus is on His way to Gethsemane. He has not yet even fought the final overcoming battle. Then He has Calvary to face. Satan and every force he can muster are determined Jesus will not make it successfully through this night. And Jesus knows it. Yet He says, "Choose peace, take courage, the battle is won!" What is that? That, my friend, is the *faith of Jesus.* That is what He means by peace, and that is what He intends will take you through every time of trouble you ever face, up to and including the final one. It's His. It's yours for the taking. He brought it in when you let Him in. Have you let Him plant it deep in the prepared and fertile soil of your heart?

Maybe peace isn't any one plant. Maybe peace is the way all the plants turn green again every spring, no matter what happens. Maybe peace is that tiny tree in the apple seed and the seeds falling from wilted, ruined flowers and baby trees growing on fallen forest giants. Maybe it's silent roots under deep snow and sap waiting, frozen, in the tree trunks. Peace is all around you, all the time. Choose it.

PATIENCE

So far, all our plants have been the kind that are scattered, growing under and over all. They have represented choices and attitudes more than actions, although love, joy, and peace, are all shown by actions, too. Now, and for the rest of the list, they will be virtues given and planted by God, but ones that we may help to grow and cultivate. It is much easier to do this if love, joy, and peace are in place and acknowledged.

First, we have good old patience. Patience is the one virtue everybody wants to have, but nobody wants to actually grow and cultivate. If only God would just hand it to us and do so quickly! We make two kinds of mistakes with patience. Either we expect God just to produce it full-grown (and when He doesn't, we say, "Well, that's just the way I am") or we try to grow it on our own.

New Year's Resolution #1: I will be more patient.

"Mommy! He hit me!"

"*Will* you two shut up! I am *trying* to write my New Year's Resolutions!"

There are different kinds of patience. The King James Version and other older Bible versions call patience "longsuffering." That would be endurance—of trials, suffering, mistreatment, or whatever. Job needed that kind of patience. People today with long-term health problems or relationship problems need that kind of patience. It's akin to peace. It means keeping our eyes on Jesus and on the end of the trail, instead of getting lost in the day-to-day traumas. It isn't easy, but it's possible, if we keep rehearsing, "Choose peace, choose courage, Jesus is in charge, and He's already overcome."

Then there is patience with people, both yourself and others. I think this has to do with expectations. All I want is to be perfect. Starting yesterday. Is that so much to ask? In my head I know how silly this is. In my head I say, "Jesus loves me just the way I am, and He's working on that, too." Yet every time I make a mistake, you can tell from my reaction that deep down I still expect to be perfect. It always shocks and dismays me when I'm not. Then you have all those other people. They're not perfect, either, have you noticed? Actually, I find it easier to be patient with other people than with myself—unless they are related to me. After all, my children, who came from my flesh, should be just as perfect as I should be.

Patient endurance, patience with yourself, patience with others. It can happen.

In her booklet *Being Your Best,** Dorothy Eaton Watts tells the story of Wilma Rudolph. Wilma had been born prematurely, then suffered two bouts with pneumonia, one with scarlet fever, and one with polio. Now she had a crooked foot and leg. The Master Gardener, with His usual love for planting where nobody thinks anything will grow, decided to plant in Wilma the desire to conquer women's sports. Sports? Why not piano or writing or something similar? No. Sports.

Wilma, twelve years old, talked her gym teacher into giving her just ten minutes a day. Believe it or not, she told the teacher that in return she would give her a world-class athlete. The teacher laughed at her, but agreed to give her the ten minutes.

Wilma took the ten minutes and opened a charge account on the patience God has in His infinite storehouse for His children. Day after day, she practiced for hours what she learned in ten minutes from a coach who didn't think she could do it. She grew to be a world-class athlete and a three-time Olympic gold medalist.

Wilma Rudolph had endurance in every sense of the word, patience with her teacher's disbelief, and patience with herself. God planted it, and together they trained it until it grew large enough to bear fruit for the whole world.

Patience is a small, slow-growing plant, not showy at all. It requires boundaries and a lot of hoeing, feeding, and coaxing. It is tender and dies quickly if neglected or subjected to harsh conditions. But the Gardener has plenty of seed, and the plant is well worth the effort, because it produces crops that will nourish not only you but everyone around you, for a lifetime.

KINDNESS

"What is desirable in a man is his kindness" (Proverbs 19:22). "She opens her mouth in wisdom, and the teaching of kindness is on her tongue" (Proverbs 31:26).

There is something attractive about the face of a kind person, isn't there? If you watch, you can see it on the street every day. The bus driver who waits an extra minute because he sees a passenger running to catch the bus. The young woman who gives up her seat to the panting, older lady when she arrives. The busy cashier who smilingly distracts a tired, fussy child while his dad digs for change. The principal who takes time to listen to the angry teenager who has been sent to the office for the third time in a week.

Kindness is an action. It is one of the ways in which patience shows itself, and both show that love, joy, and peace are planted and growing in the heart under the watchful eye of the Master Gardener. It takes deliberate choice, over and over, day after day. Perhaps more than any-thing, it takes open eyes. We have to notice the running passenger, the older lady's limp, the tired child, the cry for help in the angry teen's eyes. And we get those open eyes from spending time *that day* with Jesus, not last week or even yesterday.

Did you know pansies are also called "heartsease"? According to *Reader's Digest's* "Magic and Medicine of Plants," the traditional three colors, purple, white, and yellow, stand for memories, loving thoughts, and souvenirs. These are all ingredients of remembering to be kind. I think pansies' cheerful little faces make a perfect symbol for kindness.

GOODNESS

With my penchant for having all my thoughts neatly in a row and analytically (some say pathologically) correct, I would have put good-ness at the end if I had been the one to list the fruits of the Spirit. Love is at the top of the list, and goodness is the culmination of all those aspects of love. Of course, I am also the one who got hung up for years trying to figure out how to produce goodness at all—whether as a cul-mination or any other way.

"Only God is good," Jesus said, and He ought to know (see Mark 10:18). I repeat: *"Only God is good."*

How then, does goodness grow in our gardens? It came in with Jesus, like everything else. He plants it when He plants love, which is the other definition of *goodness.* He plants it when He plants joy and peace, which still our striving and worrying and allow us to look outward instead of inward. He plants it when He plants kindness, which makes us able to consciously choose to go out of our way to *do good* to those around us.

But God's goodness goes a step further. It enables the bus driver to still act kindly toward the passenger who swears at him, and the cashier to be patient with the customer who is out to get her fired. God's goodness has made prisoners love their abusive guards and missionaries give away their last shoes. God's goodness has caused Corrie ten Boom, tearfully, not thinking she could do it, to shake the hand of one of her former Nazi oppressors and forgive him. Forgive him! Is there anything in your past that can take you there and help you see what an impossibility that was? With God, all things are possible. Even growing goodness in my garden.

Goodness is not something I can see or measure or weed. I think it must be the combined fragrance of all the other plants in God's mini garden, deep in my heart, where every day I strive to let Him have more control and allow Him to plant more and more of whatever He wants. It's His garden.

GENTLENESS

Also known as meekness, this is a modest, unassuming plant. The person in whom God is growing gentleness and meekness is learning to regard others as more important than himself, as commanded in Philippians 2:3 and Colossians 3:12.

Gentleness is a very touchy plant to grow. If you try to plant and cultivate it yourself, you are very likely to end up with a deadly creeper called "false humility," which will kill you in one of two ways. Either you will think you are worthless, have no rights, and are here only to be abused and victimized, or you will bend all your efforts to look humble while inwardly feeling very proud of your humility. Look closely on this pretty plant, and you will find the telltale three leaves that identify the poison ivy of the spiritual world—pride. Like its natural counterpart, this is virtually impossible to kill by any power known to humanity.

It's enough to make a caretaker shy away entirely from trying to grow gentleness. But the rewards are infinite, not only here, where love will be able to have its way with us more completely, but in the next world, which the meek will inherit (see Matthew 5:5). What to do?

The secret (or one of them) appears to be found in the same text we started with—Philippians 2; however we need to read and study the context. Verses 5-8 list the steps by which Jesus grew meekness.

1. He did not *consider* or *regard* equality with God a thing to be grasped. In other words, He consciously chose to let go something that was good in itself (His equality with His Father) in order to take hold of something else (you!).

2. He emptied Himself and was made into something else. In His case, He was made human, but the point is that He allowed Himself to become whatever His Father chose.

3. He *humbled Himself to obedience, even to death.* And what was the result? Verse 9ff: He was more highly exalted than ever (see verse 9), and more important to Him, He rescued His children!

Maybe gentle meekness is like grass. It's meant to be walked on and appreciated, and it thoroughly enjoys laying itself down to be romped on by barefoot children, rolled on by babies, and rested on by weary travelers. It's not intended to be trampled, battered, or warred over. Yet instead of trying to defend itself by putting out thorns and growing high barriers, it trusts its Gardener to keep it green and thriving. It basks in His sunshine and rain, and even His mowing when necessary, knowing that He values it deeply.

FAITHFULNESS

Faithfulness can mean two different things. We usually think of faithfulness in terms of actions—fulfilling duties without skipping or shirking or having to be reminded. But it first has to mean, literally, "full of faith." And that goes all the way back to the beginning of our caretaking work in our new gardens. Once we start planting all these lovely things and have a lot to do in the daily practicalities of our spiritual growth, do we still remember that early teaching the Gardener gave us?

Do we still spend time just sitting in the sunshine of His presence, *every day?* Do we still drink the water of life all day long, and are we growing in our ability to dance in the rain He sends? Are we still remembering that *He* is the Gardener, and we are only caretakers? Or do we get caught up in trying to produce growth, even though we know perfectly well we can't do that? That's where faithfulness comes in first.

Before you can be faithful in the "little things," you have to be refilled daily with your measure of faith.

Then faithfulness becomes all kinds of things, some we've already talked of, and some we haven't. Faithfulness in love, in choosing joy and peace no matter what, in noticing people who need a little kindness, and faithfulness in whatever duties we are given. Faithfulness at work, at home, even in secret when nobody sees. It comes down to that obedience we found in Philippians 2. If God asks us to pay another ten percent besides tithe, we pay it happily. If God says our meekness needs to be mowed and hands us a lawnmower by asking us to perform some task we are tempted to think is beneath our dignity, we perform it willingly.

Faithfulness is one of those things that grows in long rows under a hot sun. Faithfulness grows blisters and muscles. But, like corn or peanuts, it and its wealth of products can feed, nurture, and support a whole community. You might not plant it in the front door yard, but you wouldn't want to be without it!

SELF-CONTROL

My trusty lexicon, in the back of *Strong's Concordance,* says that the original Greek word used here has overtones of strength, mastery, and the ability to restrain oneself, especially in matters of diet and chastity. That being the case, it seems to me that a lifetime spent working with the Master Gardener in the garden of the soul naturally produces this result.

We restrain ourselves from jogging off into the day's business before we've met with the Master and received our orders for the day. We restrain ourselves from doing what He asks us not to do, and we choose to do what He asks us to. We bring even our thoughts into subjection to Him. Then we are so filled with the delights He grows in our garden that we have no interest in less filling earthly appetites. We are too busy working in our own gardens to spend much time looking over the walls into gardens we've no business visiting, let alone playing in.

I'm not sure we notice whether or not we are growing more self-controlled. We just love to "stay in the garden with Him," and we find that "the joys we share as we tarry there, none other has ever known."

There's an element of self-control that must not be overlooked. That is the need to be temperate in good things. We are aware of all the things we shouldn't do, but sometimes we overdo and even kill ourselves doing things we should do, but that we shouldn't try to do all at once or accomplish all by ourselves. Pay attention, and the Gardener will keep you in balance in all the areas of your life.

Self-control can be exemplified in our inner gardens as the work we do alongside the Gardener. He planted it when He first gave you that child-sized trowel and let you help Him dig out the new spring the Holy Spirit had opened in your heart. He develops it every time He asks you to mow down some meekness, prune some skill that's taking over your life because you can't say "No," put on heavy gloves and grub out some weeds, or trim a bag full of love starts and give them away to grow in someone else's life.

A REMINDER AND A WARNING

I've said it before, and I'll probably say it again, because we human caretakers get off the track so easily. God is the Gardener. Never plant or work without Him. Ezekiel 17 tells a parable that should be studied in its entirety. It shows how a terrible event, the Babylonian captivity, was part of the Master Gardener's plan, and how those who tried to resist it and turned to Egypt for help, ruined everything, although it seemed like a wise political move. God had actually delegated Babylon to transplant a cedar shoot from Jerusalem, and God declared that when that shoot grew strong and sent out shoots toward Egypt, it would be torn up by the roots and its fruit cut off. If we try to plant anything—*anything*—in our lives contrary to God's plan or if we try to grow what He has planted in a different direction than He has planned for it, we are in grave danger.

However, Ezekiel 17 ends with hope and promises. "Thus says the Lord God, 'I shall also take a sprig from the lofty top of the cedar and set it out; I shall pluck from the topmost of its young twigs a tender one, and I shall plant it on a high and lofty mountain. On the high mountain of Israel I shall plant it, that it may bring forth boughs and bear fruit, and become a stately cedar. And birds of every kind will nest under it; they will nest in the shade of its branches. And all the trees of the field will know that I am the Lord; I bring down the high tree, exalt the low tree, dry up the green tree, and make the dry tree flourish. I am the Lord; I have spoken, and I will perform it' " (verses 22-24).

God continues the same theme in Ezekiel 36:34-36. " 'The desolate land will be cultivated instead of being a desolation in the sight of everyone who passed by. And they will say, "This desolate land has become like the garden of Eden; and the waste, desolate, and ruined cities are fortified and inhabited." Then the nations that are left round about you will know that I, the Lord, have rebuilt the ruined places and planted that which was desolate; I, the Lord, have spoken and will do it.' "

He will do it. And when He does, everyone will see. And they will magnify His name.

DIG DEEPER

Spend some time looking again at the list of fruit in Galatians 5:22, 23 and asking God how He is growing these in you. Ask Him if there are ways He would like to plant more. If you have some areas where there is a lack of cooperation, turn them over to Him and watch for the miracles.

Colossians 3 is another beautiful chapter about the qualities God wants to grow in His children. In this passage, clothing is the imagery used; there are things to "put off" and things to "put on." Study this passage and write down the wonderful characteristics that God is giving *you* by His grace. Praise His name!

In describing the growth of the mustard seed, which represents faith, Jesus says that the birds of the air will rest in its branches. This is a foreshadowing of the goal He has for you and me—that our faith will not only strengthen and nurture ourselves, but that it will provide shelter for those weaker than we are or for those who are in need of whatever help we can provide. You will find further inspiration for this goal in the following passages: Psalm 104:12; Ezekiel 17:23; 31:6; 4:12. What are the similarities and differences in these passages and in their contexts? What lessons can you learn?

Snapshots From My Garden

She stood in the center of her garden, near the Tree, and turned in slow circles. How long had it been since she had stood here mourning dirt and aching muscles? How long since she thought there was no progress? Her muscles were strong now and rarely complained. She turned toward the crystal gate. It shimmered beneath a white latticed arbor, with seats on each side, pastel vines twining overhead, and bright blossoms at its feet. She now had a few friends who met her there regularly. She turned toward the eastern wall, which was built higher than the walls of the other sides and was always warm because it faced the afternoon sun. Seed beds were there, and young whips of fruit trees. On the northeast corner of the wall, ivy was beginning to climb the watchtower. She turned northward, and right before her, under the Tree and next to the spring, was the secret place she shared with her Gardener. It had become a blessed grotto, with ferns and shy flowers, ivy and moss, and the sound of tinkling water. That swing was more precious to her than it had ever been. She turned west and saw neat beds of greens and early vegetables in the wide, clear space away from the afternoon shade of the wall.

A deep, contented sigh escaped her. There was still one mystery, though. In a warm corner, the Gardener had built large wire enclosures and had showed her how to layer within them weeds, dirt, leftover vegetable and fruit peels, the leaves of certain plants, and water. It was hard, but rather interesting. He had assured her that the heaps of useless garbage they had accumulated in weeks of hard work were not useless at all, but would be a treasure trove when treated correctly.

The Gardener was there now, turning the whole mound with His fork, so she joined Him. She didn't ask what He was doing. He turned the whole thing frequently. She got a fork and helped Him, enjoying the companionable labor even though she had no clue what it was about. Then He stuck His fork deeply into the pile and pulled it out full.

"Look," He said, smiling as if a goal had been met.

She looked. His fork was full of rich dirt. She looked up at His face. She still didn't understand.

"This isn't dirt," said the Gardener. "This is called compost. It is packed full of nutrients—food for our new plants and for your tree."

"You mean, that's what all these weeds and garbage turned into?"

"Exactly. Before, they were a problem. Now they are part of the solution." His grin was infectious.

She laughed. "That's incredible! I can hardly believe it! How does it happen?"

He laughed too. "Well, I could explain the scientific process to you, and you could learn to understand it, in a way. But the bottom line is, this is one of the unsearchable things My Father, the Spirit, and I do, and you'll never really know how, anymore than you know how life or growth happens."

"So what do we do now?" she asked.

"Now we refill the wheelbarrow again with this transformed stuff and put it back where we found it—in the garden. Only now, instead of rotting, or growing rank and stealing water and nutrients, it will feed our plants and help them to conserve water.

She worked with Him—they were good partners now—and dug in the compost, piling it around roots and under plants or along rows. As she worked, she wondered. It seemed like a miracle. She guessed it was. Bad things changed into good things. Well, when she thought of it, that was what He always did. She hummed as she used her hands to edge compost under the small flowers at the gate.

Some friends saw her there and came to ask questions. She explained what the Gardener had told her, and they were amazed, too. "You mean, He'll turn my weeds into helpful things in my garden?"

She grinned at them. "He will. In fact, He's probably already started, and you don't even know it. That's how He works, you know."

They grinned back. They knew.

That evening, in the swing, the Gardener told her, "It's still not a perfect world, remember. The compost will make weeds grow too. We will have to be vigilant."

More work? It didn't scare her as much as it used to.

"Vigilant," she whispered to herself. She liked the sound of it. Watchful, like the tower. She leaned on His shoulder and left it for tomorrow.

CHAPTER 10

Feeding and Watering: The Nurture and Admonition of the Lord

" 'The kingdom of God is like a man who casts seed upon the soil; and goes to bed at night and gets up by day, and the seed sprouts up and grows—how, he himself does not know. The soil produces crops by itself; first the blade, then the head, then the mature grain in the head. But when the crop permits, he immediately puts in the sickle, because the harvest has come' " (Mark 4:26-29).

This parable reminds us that even in real life, we have no idea how a garden grows. It's like magic, which is why you're "nearer God's heart" there than anywhere else on earth. In spiritual life, growth is even more of a mystery. We recognize only the harvest—and sometimes not even that. But God sees every blade and every grain, every molecular bit of growth.

In the crucial subject of the care and feeding of what God plants (also called "working out what God works in"), it can get really tricky figuring out what is our work and what is God's. Is God giving me patience or is it my practice that makes perfect? Would it do any good for me to simply decide to grow patience, without benefit of God's seeds? No. But, then, how effective is it for me to beg daily for patience, but refuse to practice it? In this chapter we will study what God and we can do together to develop the qualities He has planted in us.

Isaiah gives a graphic picture of God hovering daily over His gardens. " 'A vineyard of wine, sing of it! I, the Lord, am its keeper; I water it every moment. Lest anyone damage it, I guard it night and day. I have no wrath. Should someone give Me briars and thorns in battle, then I would step on them, I would burn them completely. Or let him rely on My protection, let him make peace with Me, let him make peace with Me.' In the days to come Jacob will take root, Israel will blossom and sprout; and they will fill the whole world with fruit" (Isaiah 27:2-6). Meditate on this scene and put your name into these promises. Accept them. God is caring for you, watering you *"every moment"*! He is not mad at you! If you fight Him and give Him thorns and briars, He'll get rid of them, but He'd so much rather you make peace with Him and work together. Then your fruit will fill your corner of your world, and together, you'll fill the earth with rejoicing in the Master Gardener's bounty.

If you remain open to His leading, God will enrich your ground still further, so that what He has planted will grow abundantly. Psalm 65:9, 10 sings it this way:

> Thou dost visit the earth, and cause it to overflow;
> Thou dost greatly enrich it;
> The stream of God is full of water;
> Thou dost prepare their grain, for thus Thou dost prepare the earth.
> Thou dost water its furrows abundantly;
> Thou dost settle its ridges;
> Thou dost soften it with showers;
> Thou dost bless its growth.

And if there's something in you that is weak and trembling, about to die, God knows how to deal with that, too. " 'A bruised reed He will not break' " (Isaiah 42:3). Even though you have allowed the Spirit to cause His everlasting spring to break forth into your life, are there still reeds there that are hovering on the edge of failure? Turn them over without reserve to the Master Gardener. And start consciously watering.

In my vegetable garden, a wonderful thing has happened. My husband put in a standing, frost-free hydrant! I have water! Right there! Now I'll never have to water again! Right? Wrong. I still have to hook up the hose and take the water to where it's needed in my large garden. Not only that, I plan to build a new chicken house nearby, and I will need to take water to the chickens and even more to the ducks and geese for the little swimming pool they love so much.

So it is in our spiritual gardens. The Spirit comes in the minute He's asked; don't ever let anyone, not even your doubting self, tell you differently. Then begins the lifelong task of consciously opening up different areas of your life (which God will show you as you grow) to that life-giving water. Do you consciously drink of the Spirit before you speak to your spouse or child who has hurt you? Do you drink of Him before you make a business deal? When you fill out your tax return? Even when you choose or work at a hobby? He wants to water *all* areas of your life every moment.

And here's another point. Proverbs 11:25 says, "The generous man will be prosperous, and he who waters will himself be watered." If this is true of temporal sharing, how much more true it must be of spiritual sharing! When you find the water of life, you share it, and as you share it, it grows deeper and flows more fully in yourself.

Elaine was wavering on the brink of depression. Her husband had died, she had no visible means of support, and the whole world seemed gray and dry. She felt as if she had died when Gerald died. When her doctor talked her into trying a grief-management group, she agreed very reluctantly. Grief management! The very term seemed contrived and false. Step one, step two, step three—as easily measured as waste water management. Did somebody get a degree in this—Dr. So-and-So, G.M.— and could they now make Elaine's sorrow fall away like a snake's old skin?

At the first meeting, Elaine said nothing. But she learned that there were people here who felt as she did, and more important, she learned that some were now getting better, slowly. She went back. And then she learned something that changed her life. She met Ann, whose husband had died more recently than Elaine's, and who still couldn't speak without crying. Elaine began to reach out to try to comfort Ann, and found that when they talked together and cried together, she felt better, too. After a while, life began to look manageable again. She realized this was what they meant by "grief management." Grief wouldn't go away until she met Gerald again in God's arms, but it could become manageable. Livable. And she and Ann could help each other.

So you consciously carry the water God gives you to all parts of your own garden, and when you can, you share it with others. When they're willing, lead them to the Source, so they too will have an everlasting spring in all the vicissitudes of life.

Then there's feeding and fertilizing. We spoke at some length in an earlier chapter about the way God often uses harsh circumstances or events to enrich us. But it isn't the troubles themselves that make us strong. Anne Morrow Lindberg is said to have pointed out that if suffering always made people strong, we would *all* be incredibly strong. It's what you choose to do with the suffering that makes the difference.

When I learned about year-around composting—instead of weeding and tilling—as a gardening method, I wondered about the spiritual application. (I tend to think everything has a spiritual application. That's one way I practice the presence of God.) We've been raised on sermons about pulling out each tiny weed of sin before it gets too big and deep rooted. When you compost, you bury the soil so deep under other weeds and garbage that (ideally) weeds can't grow to begin with. I got to thinking that if weeds are sin, this seemed to imply that sin could enrich our lives. That couldn't be right!

But the more I thought about it and looked at my experience in that light, the more I realized that all our worst weaknesses are usually our best traits turned inside out and twisted out of shape. Satan can't create on his own. He has to take what God has made and mutate it. I began to see that it is true that in my life God does use the composting method! He takes my weaknesses as well as my troubles, chops them up, and mixes them with His grace, turns and turns them in His Word, and actually reduces them elementally into something entirely different—

something that can nourish and transform me. Guess who gets to turn the pile? Guess what happens to the whole mess when I forget to turn it? Bible study is one of the most essential ways to feed the soul, and it's something we can do.

In 1 Corinthians 3, Paul says, "And I, brethren, could not speak to you as to spiritual men, but as to men of flesh, as to babes in Christ. I gave you milk to drink, not solid food; for you were not yet able to receive it" (verses 1, 2). In Hebrews 6 he defines what he means by "spiritual milk"—food for new Christians. He says the foundation of our spiritual understanding is to be based in "repentance from dead works and of faith toward God" (verse 1). That is, that we can't, and mustn't try, to work our way to heaven or to God's favor; we must receive righteousness entirely by faith. Then he mentions "instruction about washings, and laying on of hands" (verse 2), which would represent teachings about church rituals and ceremonies, baptism, ordination, etc. And finally, "the resurrection of the dead, and eternal judgment" (verse 2). Obviously, these are basic things new Christians must learn. Paul calls them the milk of the Word.

New Christians tend to learn these things from their pastors or more experienced Christian friends. But if you are a new Christian, let me encourage you to begin right away to learn to feed yourself. Look up these topics and prayerfully consider them. What do you really believe, and why do you believe it? Can you defend it? Your pastor and friends stand ready to help you, but they are also eager to see you learning for yourself. Paul sounds impatient with those who still need milk, but the risen Jesus specifically called Peter to feed the new lambs (see John 21:15-17). Here is Peter's tender invitation: "Therefore, putting aside all malice and all guile and hypocrisy and envy and all slander, like newborn babes, long for the pure milk of the word, that by it you may grow in respect to salvation, if you have tasted the kindness of the Lord" (1 Peter 2:1-3).

As you grow, you'll be ready for meat, or solid food. Believe me, there is enough in the Bible to fill the appetite of every human for a very long lifetime! In the context of the passages in 1 Corinthians 3 and Hebrews 5 alone, we find the nature and work of the Holy Spirit, the foundation and reward of human works in God, our souls as temples of God, the deep study of the sanctuary system, the high-priestly work of Christ, the human/divine nature of Christ, and the old and new covenants. And that list reflects just a skimming perusal of these chapters!

Physically, our bodies are at some point in the digestive cycle literally all the time. We are either eating, digesting, or resting and assimilating, getting ready for the next meal. Why is it that we think we can live for a week at a time, or even longer, without spiritual food? Is it any wonder that our spiritual lives become weak and listless? Wouldn't your body be weak if you ate only once a week or less? Wouldn't you, in fact, die?

You and your Master Gardener are building that inner garden for a purpose. It is to feed and nurture you and those around you. Determine that you will spend time daily chewing on real meat from the Word of God. Listen to the words and teachings of others, too, but don't depend on them. Rightly divide the Word yourself. As Paul said, "I planted, and Apollos watered, but God was causing the growth. So then neither the one who plants nor the one who waters is anything, but God who causes the growth.... For we are God's fellow workers; you are God's field, God's building" (1 Corinthians 3:6, 9).

If you ever find yourself forgetting where the bread comes from, reread John 6. Talk about a heavy meal! This chapter tells of the watershed experience in Jesus' ministry. He had been telling stories for quite a while, feeding the multitudes with milk. On this day, He tried solid food. He said *He* was the Bread and Water and Manna of life. He said that unless they ate His flesh and drank His blood, they were dead! Most of His listeners promptly spit out what He offered. So many of "His disciples" left Him that Jesus sadly turned to His special twelve and asked, "Will you leave Me too?" Peter answered with a very good question: "Leave You and go where?" (see John 6:66-69).

So we have learned that we can consciously water our souls with the power and presence of the Holy Spirit, and that we must feed our souls on the Word of God. There is one more thing, and it is probably the hardest of all. It involves a decision of the will and attitude. Paul says, "Even so *consider yourselves to be dead to sin,* but alive to God in Christ Jesus" (Romans 6:11, emphasis supplied). I warn you, this is a chewy passage. I recommend you study the whole chapter, and the surrounding chapters, and . . . well, you get the picture. But here's where I'm going with it in this chapter: *What you pay attention to (what you consider to be true) is what will grow.*

This is *so easy* to get backward! When I pray, "Oh, Lord, I have such a terrible temper! Please take away this terrible temper! I know I don't honor You when I give way to my terrible temper. Please help me not to have a terrible temper anymore. . . ." What am I paying attention to? What (I speak from experience) will grow? What do I believe about myself? What I believe about myself is invariably true, you know. That's the way God made us (see Proverbs 23:7).

In an earlier chapter we talked about cultivation and that it means to practice, train, refine, tend, etc. Here is where you begin to be able to train and shape what God has planted in you, to have some choices, as caretaker. We have seen that God, as Master Gardener, has made His choices. He has planted some absolutes in your life—virtues that you chose by default when you chose Him, that you couldn't say No to without saying No to Him. These include, among other things, the fruits of the Spirit listed in Galatians 5. The Gardener also had a master plan for each of our lives by the time we were born—or before.

But He often gives us some choices when it comes to specifics. Take our lifework, for example. You might say this is represented by the over-all style of our garden. God usually seems to design us for one certain type of work. We have the talents and gifts and end up with the train-ing, (one way or another) for, let's say, a teaching career. Then when the job offers come, sometimes it seems clear that He's sending us to one specific place; other times He seems to give us a choice. He asks, "Do you want to work in Tennessee or British Columbia? Do you want to teach elementary school for Me or be a school principal?"

God designed me to be a writer; I knew that by the age of nine. So I knew the "what," and I soon figured out the "why"—to share the love of God with everybody I could reach. The "how," "when," and "where" took a lot longer to develop! He had chosen me to be a writer, but I had some choices to make as well, and still do, daily.

Let's say some of the individual plants represent specific talents. God planted them in your garden, but in some ways, they may be subject to your choice. For example, God says to you, "I made you to be musical. Do you want to play the flute or the piano or sing? Or all three?" Whatever you pick, guess who has to do the daily practicing? God will give you the talent, the will, and it is God's magical work in your body that will enable your brain and fingers and vocal cords to learn the awesome and incredible things they have to learn. But you decide whether to practice or not.

God planted a little musical ability in my heart's garden. Among other things, I've wanted to play the piano my whole life. When I was a child, the question was whether we would have enough to eat, clothes to wear, and a roof over our heads. Pianos and lessons did not enter the equation. Finally, in my early twenties, I was blessed with a $25 piano. I was thrilled and played all the time. I learned to play a few chords with my left hand and pick out a melody with one finger of the right.

Then I decided I wanted to really learn. I bought a piano book and started at page one. Due to physical conditions beyond my control, I have fairly poor coordination. My progress was slow and discouraging. I picked my way through the little pieces, but I skipped all the boring scales and finger exercises, and especially the written exercises. Strangely enough, I never really did learn to play. In fact, even if I practiced a piece fifty times, I was so bad that I gave up and decided I would play in heaven.

God had done the planting. He and I were supposed to do the care and feeding together. I reneged on my part of the bargain. But I never kicked out the Gardener, and He kept that tiny, stunted plant alive and nagging at my heart. When I finally grew up (I consider true adulthood to kick in around age forty, and no, I'm not kidding), I said to myself, "Who said you have to be Horowitz?" The old piano was long defunct, so I got an inexpensive keyboard and dug out my old books. This time I didn't skip the exercises and scales. I began to progress, but still slowly. Finally, last year, I found a piano teacher. I said, "Pretend I know nothing at all and start me out as if I were a child. We'll find the gaps and work on them."

My teacher is wonderful and demanding, and *she thinks I can do it.* Slowly, she's convincing me, too, that I can do it. She also knows what she's doing. I do runs and scales and arpeggios and write out theory lessons. I learn technique pieces. I practice at least half an hour almost every day, and often more. I'm still uncoordinated. I still wouldn't give Horowitz a run for his money. But I played a piano solo at our church's Christmas program this past year. And I'm working on the "Moonlight Sonata" (although *not* in its difficult original key—yet!). Most exciting of all to me, my obedience in another area—in settling down to my lifework and ministry of writing—has now bought me a beautiful, gently used Baldwin piano!

Here's one of the most important things my piano teacher is teaching me. When I pay attention to the mistakes and worry over them, I play terribly. When I pay attention to the music, and play for the love of it, I play much better. This may be one of the single most vital things I can learn in my spiritual life, as well.

Don't pray about your temper. Pray about patience, and a gentle spirit, and *believe Him when He promises them to you.*

Don't pray about your laziness. Pray about diligence. Learn promises of diligence. Practice believing you can be diligent.

Don't pray about your cancer. Pray about health, both physical and spiritual, which is the only kind that really counts in the end. This life is temporary, anyway. Learn and practice healthful living, and don't forget that one of the "natural doctors" is trust in God.

Consider yourself—reckon yourself, count yourself, believe yourself—*dead to sin and alive to Christ.* Practice that certainty and the certainty of His presence. Cultivate and train love and joy and peace.

> And [you] shall come and shout for joy on the height of Zion,
> And [you] shall be radiant over the bounty of the Lord—
> Over the grain, and the new wine, and the oil,
> And over the young of the flock and the herd;
> And [your] life shall be like a watered garden,
> And [you] shall never languish again
> (Jeremiah 31:12).

DIG DEEPER

List some areas of your soul that you know need water. Ask the Holy Spirit to show you how to open those to His life-giving water and what you can do every day to drink of Him. Write down your decisions and stick to them, remembering always to do them *with* God, not by yourself.

Think or write about some times in your life when others have shared their water with you, and times when you have shared the water of life with others. What were the results?

What is your worst weakness? Think about it and decide whether it's a strength turned inside out. Then ask God to compost it back into the elemental strength He intended it to be. Have you ever seen Him turn a weakness into a strength? Have you seen Him take away a strength that was destructive, and make it weak and powerless over you?

Are you studying milk or meat? Think seriously about where you are in your spiritual life and whether you really have had all the milk you need. If you haven't, don't go on to meat until you are sure of the basics. Try to learn to study the Bible by yourself, just you and God, rather than depending on other humans. If you are ready for meat, what would you like to study? If you are a mature Christian, what meat will you chew on next? Note: If you are a mature Christian, watch carefully for self-satisfaction or a lack of dependence on God. In one way, we're all still babies, and it's dangerous to forget it!

When and how do you do your deep Bible study?

Name some sins in your life, pull them out, and practice considering them dead as dust under your feet. Look at Jesus, not at those old faults!

What are some of the talents and desires that God has given you? When has He given you choices, and how has He blessed them? What are some choices you are making right now, or in the near future? How will you decide?

Snapshots From My Garden

She meant to be vigilant, and at first she was. She hoed and raked minuscule weeds by the hundreds. If she missed some until they got bigger, she pulled them and laid them roots up in the row, where they dried out and became part of the mulch. But the garden was now growing so beautiful and so enjoyable that it became more difficult to work, and more desirable to lie around or swing or sit under the arbor with her new friends. Some mornings, she went there instead of meeting her Gardener in their grotto under the Tree.

She felt she was becoming almost an expert, and now loved to answer the questions her friends asked. Sometimes they brought new people, and she told her whole story over again. Over time, the story changed a little, without her noticing it. Her original structure wasn't quite so hodgepodge and desperate. The Gardener came at her request, and was more of a helper than a leader. She dispensed advice freely and delighted in hearing the success stories her friends shared after they took her advice. They really didn't have to hire the Gardener themselves. She was perfectly willing to share all that He taught her.

The sun shone, and the silver rains fell, and the plants in the garden grew tall and lush and began to bloom. It was more crowded than it had been. She realized she'd better get to work on some of those weeds. There was one vine in particular that had begun to climb the wall in several places. She wondered at first if it really was a weed; it was quite pretty, with glossy green leaves in trios. She decided to leave it. Perhaps she could even feed it. It might have beautiful blossoms if it were given some attention. She put some compost around its roots and pulled some weeds, but they were strong and hard to uproot now. Most of the time, they just broke off. Well, at least the garden looked better. Tired and frustrated, she soon quit.

She was lingering at the gate the next morning when one of her oldest friends came by. "Good morning, Grace!" she greeted her eagerly. "I haven't seen you in a while!"

"Well," said her friend, "I came by a few times, but you always looked busy. Why are you scratching your arms like that?"

"Oh, it's nothing. Just a rash. I think the Gardener told me one of the plants around here is good for rashes."

"Where is the Gardener?" asked Grace.

She looked around and shrugged. "I don't know. I haven't seen that much of Him lately. He's probably busy. There's plenty for both of us to do now. My garden is growing beautifully, as you can see!" She smiled with pride.

Grace looked uncomfortable.

"What's the matter?" she demanded. "Don't you think my garden is beautiful?"

"Yes, of course, but . . . Well, for one thing, I thought you said it was His garden now."

"Well, of course it is! It's our garden!" What on earth was Grace trying to lead up to? It sounded suspiciously like criticism! She scratched irritably.

"It's not for me to tell you how to grow your garden," said her friend gently. "It's just that I think it was prettier when you and the Gardener worked together more. You spend so much time at the gate now. And the other day, when I came by and you were telling the story again. . . . Well, I don't want to hurt you, truly I don't, but it seemed the story wasn't quite the way you told it to me."

"First of all, we do work together!" She was trying to remain patient, but it wasn't easy. "He is the One who convinced me I needed to have friends and to spend time with them. I can't do everything, you know! Second, I tell that story exactly the way it happened! I was there! You weren't!"

Grace backed away sadly. "I know. I'm sorry. I don't mean to . . . Well, I just think you should talk to the Gardener, that's all. And ask Him about that rash too. It looks serious to me. Goodbye."

"Goodbye! And thanks so much for your kind advice!" she called crossly, turning back into her garden.

From a little distance, Grace turned and called to her, "I love you! I hope you believe that!"

For an answer, she slammed the gate.

The Gardener found her crying in a corner. Without saying anything, He gathered her up and took her to the spring, where He washed her rash in the water, then mashed some fresh green herbs and spread them on it. There was some relief immediately.

When she could speak a little, she thanked Him and gulped, "How did it happen?"

"That pretty vine on your wall is Pride. The rash, which will take some time to heal, is the least of the trouble it causes. It is the most terrible of all plants, so powerful for evil that it can't even be composted."

She sniffed, feeling like a first-class idiot. "Oh. So I should have pulled it."

"No. You shouldn't have touched it. You should have left it to Me."

"Then why didn't You do something about it?"

He looked at her. "Lately, you've seemed to prefer working in your garden alone."

She flung herself on His chest, weeping anew. "No! No, I haven't, really! I'm so sorry! I've made a mess of things again!"

"I forgive you. Together, we can bring order back."

He held her, rocking gently, and she realized how much she had missed Him. After a while, she murmured into His shoulder, "You sent Grace to talk to me, didn't You?"

When He nodded, she asked, "From now on, will You come with me when I meet with my friends?"

She could feel the warmth of His smile without looking up. "I thought you'd never ask!"

CHAPTER 11

Weeding: Giving Up What God Digs Out

If you garden, you know that one of the most frustrating things is that the more you till and compost and enrich and water . . . the more the weeds will love you! They grow as lush and beautiful as any pampered rose or artichoke or strawberry. And the more you enrich and cultivate your spiritual and devotional life, the more you will notice character defects you never saw before. Nineteenth-century author Ellen White went so far as to say that the closer we come to Christ, the worse we'll look to ourselves! (see *Steps to Christ,* pp. 64, 65). This could be pretty discouraging, but she says the solution is not to look at ourselves, but at Jesus. The view is immeasurably better, and what we see is, literally, what we get. His character qualities become ours as we behold them. Unbelievable!

God knew there would be weeds, and He doesn't seem to get as discouraged about them as I do. He simply says that " 'instead of the thorn bush the cypress will come up; and instead of the nettle the myrtle will come up; and it will be a memorial to the Lord, for an everlasting sign which will not be cut off' " (Isaiah 55:13). Clearly, the Master Gardener has a plan. The question, then, is how can we caretakers help and not hinder Him?

In this chapter, we'll take a look at several different kinds of weeds and the differing controls each will need. Some "weeds" are actually useful plants when they're under control. They can be used either as mulch or compost, or actually be grown as garden plants, under the correct conditions. Other weeds are deadly and must be eradicated. The Bible actually speaks of some people as being weeds that must be totally destroyed! What is God talking about, and how can we be certain never to be included in that category?

In the last chapter, I mentioned that I've found God often takes my weaknesses, which I thought were all bad, and transforms them into something valuable for my soul's nourishment. I called it God's compost pile. Let me give some specific examples.

Peter was a brash, self-opinionated, fast-talking sailor. When he fell, he fell hard. Judas Iscariot was more sophisticated, but just as self-opinionated and just as sure he was right. Both of them tried to tell Jesus how He ought to run His "campaign." Both of them betrayed Him on the last day of His life.

Jesus loved them both. He reached out to them both. When He said gently to Judas, "Can you betray Me with a kiss?" (see Luke 22:28), Judas didn't break down and weep and repent. He chose to turn away, still certain he was right and would be proven so in the end. But Jesus had only to look at Peter, and Peter's repentance was so deep he never forgot it. Then Jesus took the weaknesses of Peter's character and made them into strengths that the other disciples didn't have. Peter was the tender one you needed if you had a bruised soul in need of healing. Peter's weeds, dug up, given to the Master, wrapped in His grace, and ripened for a time, became just the compost he needed. So did the other disciples' weeds, of course. Everybody's weeds are different.

A woman who has failed in her marriage can be of immeasurable help to other struggling ones—if she's had her weeds thoroughly composted by Jesus. If not, she'll either be bitter or tell her women friends, "Go ahead, dump the creep! I've never been so happy!"

A man who used to be a drug addict and gang member can reach and rescue drug addicts and gang members. Or he can preach far and wide about his "past" perversity until the kids who listen to him want to be just like him in every way—drugs and gangs included.

If you try to dig up every weed you have, making a list, perhaps, as Benjamin Franklin is said to have done, you'll find each one leaves behind several pieces of root that grow into ten more weeds. Be sure you dig only with the Master Gardener and that you give any and all weeds to Him to be buried in His grace, so that all you see is Him and His blinding goodness. Then you and your weeds will be transformed into something that can nourish not only you, but others as well.

Then there are the weeds—like dandelion or mint—which are really helpful plants out of control or in the wrong place. They're great plants. But they sure take over a garden or lawn if you let them!

Lila is a helper. She doesn't need to take a Spiritual Gifts Inventory to know she has the gift of helping. She loves to help! She's loved to help since she was a little girl. If you need anything done, anything at all, just call Lila. She never says No. She practically runs the church, the school, her community, and of course her own home and family. At work she doesn't get the promotions she really deserves, when you consider that the whole place would fall apart without her. But Lila doesn't mind, because she's nothing if not self-sacrificing. Everybody but Lila can see that if she doesn't learn to say No, she's headed for the hospital. Or the mental ward.

Then there's my own personal favorite weed. When I neglect my soul's garden, (or the one outside, for that matter!) it's generally for one reason—procrastination. This is one of those ubiquitous weeds in everyone's garden, but some of us grow more of a bumper crop than others. When you procrastinate, it's not because you want to do wrong. It's not even that you *don't* want to do right. It's just . . . Well, let's be crystal clear. It's love of ease based on a total misperception of what is easy! I, for one, would rather finish reading my book than go outside and hoe corn! It's easier. Isn't it? If I made the superhuman effort of actually getting off the sofa and out into the sunshine, I would soon be full of energy and delightedly scraping away in soft soil with gazillions of teensy weeds in it. In a half-hour, I could do the whole sweet-corn patch. I could probably still come in and finish my book, but who wants to read on a day like this? I'd spread a thick mulch between the corn rows, tie up some tomatoes, and thin some carrots, and . . . you get the picture.

If, on the other hand, I stay inside and read, it'll be easier to stay inside tomorrow and the next day, and then it will rain, and when the garden is dry enough to work again, it will take me an hour of sweaty, back-breaking effort to hack the weeds out of one or two rows of corn. There will be no point in mulching, because the weeds' root systems, hale and hearty by now, are still there, and like mulch as much as corn does. In my experience, unless you use black plastic and two feet of straw, the weeds will still find a way out. By this time, I will have a headache, the tomatoes will be sprawling on the ground, the carrots will be a jungle, and . . . get the picture? *Which would have been easier— to deal with the weeds early on or to procrastinate?*

Then there's the checkbook. Which is easier—to balance the checkbook in five minutes at the end of the month (ten minutes if you made a math error) or to take the whole embarrassing mess to the bank to sort out, six months, three check-return charges, and nobody knows how many math errors later?

Here's my shocking conclusion: Procrastination is really inertia— that is, the desire to keep on doing what you're doing instead of changing, and it's one of the physical laws God built into the universe. Really! Look it up. *Once, by the grace of God, I make the effort and get out into the garden, inertia (procrastination) is on my side!* I want to keep on gardening until it gets too dark to see or the mosquitoes drive me in. And once you make the decision to get in the habit of working with the Master in your soul's garden, it will be hard to quit, too.

Some might accuse me here of saying that sin makes us stronger. I've had some angst over that, myself. It cannot be true that we will be closer to God when this dreadful detour is over than we would have been if Eve had simply stuck with Adam or told the serpent to get lost! But here we are. And in this broken world, with the broken natures we have here, God uses trouble and pain and sometimes even sin—none of which would ever have begun if it were up to Him, and none of which He creates or causes—to teach, strengthen, and nourish us. That's the truth now, whether it was ever intended to be that way, or not.

Perhaps it will help to look for a moment at the difference between *Sin* and *sins*. The procrastination, betrayals, unloving acts, drug addictions, etc. that we've talked about in this book are all *sins*. Sins are actions that are wrong, caused by choices that are wrong. Sometimes they are well-intentioned. God can and does use them (transformed by His grace) as "compost" in our lives. *Sin,* on the other hand, is that brokenness within us, that nature we have that leads to the wrong choices, that root of all the evil that ever was or ever will be. *Sin* kills. It killed God, and it will kill us if we don't give it to Him.

Sins, wrong acts, are what we tend to look at in order to decide how close to perfect we are. News flash: if you could succeed in never doing a wrong act for the rest of your life, you would still not be perfect! You would still be a sinner. Because *Sin* is not what you do, it's who you are. With Adam and Eve's sin, we were cursed to inherit sin, and nothing will change that until Jesus comes and changes our natures.

Another news flash (a better one): when you said Yes to Jesus, He gave you a new nature. Not just *a* new nature, *His* totally sinless nature. That is as perfect as they come. But while we live on this earth, this new nature will still be in old vessels, and there will still be occasional splits and spills.

So when I refer to sins as weeds and talk about God using some sins to help us, and about some sins that have to be destroyed, I hope I don't confuse you. All *Sin* (*sins* too) will be destroyed, and my garden allegory will never perfectly reflect perfect truth any more than any other human perception does. It's useful only as a dim reflection of the face and acts of God in our lives.

I want to look at the *Sin* that is the poison ivy of the spiritual world—pride, the root of all sin. Pride can't be composted. Pride can't be pruned or trimmed or trained or confined. It can't even be touched. And *you* can't get rid of it. It keeps coming back. It looks quite pretty, especially in its fall colors. You can think it's OK as long as it's over there, out of the way. And the birds like the berries. Forget it. Pride is what got us all into this mess in the first place. Lucifer got to thinking what a great being he was, and everything went downhill from there.

You could say that even pride has its positive root, because God does want us to love, appreciate, and care for ourselves. He's the One who made Lucifer beautiful and wise. It's difficult to discuss this subject clearly because in our language the word *pride* has a lot of different meanings, some of them good. But a joyful, contented sense of self-worth in Christ is totally different from the self-idolatry, the Pride with a capital P, that is the root of all sin. The former will come automatically from His love, joy, and peace. You can't keep one sprig of the latter. It's all got to go.

How? By putting on heavy gloves, watching carefully for it, and grubbing out every sign of it that you see? No! Remember, what you pay attention to is what grows. How then? It's impossible! Luckily for us, what is impossible with us is entirely possible with God.

"He answered and said, 'Every plant which My heavenly Father did not plant shall be rooted up. Let them alone' " (Matthew 15:13, 14). Note: I took this passage out of context, so be sure to look it up and read the whole thing. I think you'll see the principle, just the same.

You do your job, and let God do His! He is the Gardener; you are only the caretaker. That means your job is to take care of things. Pay attention to what you do want, not what you don't want. What is God planting in your life? Do you find love, faithfulness, and peace growing in your garden? Tend them carefully. Spend your daily time with Him in the sun and the rain. Feed what He tells you to, carry the water where He sends you, mow when He asks you to, and yes, grub out weeds *when He tells you to*. Just yesterday, He had me grub out a sprig of pride I hadn't noticed. I was a little taken aback. "But . . . that's not really pride, is it?" I asked.

"Yes it is," He said.

I pulled it and gave it to Him. It was surprisingly easy, after a minute. But talking about it makes me eye it again, a little longingly. So I think

I'll stop and turn to a story that illustrates the same thing—the story of the wheat and the tares, found in Matthew 13:24-43.

To a gardener, this is an amazing story. Leave the weeds there and let them grow? You've got to be kidding! Now, of course, as Jesus Himself explains, He is speaking of people—the good and the wicked—and explaining why He doesn't just give everybody what they deserve right now. Because, He points out (see verse 29), some of the supposed "good guys" would get it too. Oh. Well, in that case . . . Come to think of it, I don't want what I deserve. Every single one of us is a weed patch deserving of burning. The day will come when all weed patches will be destroyed. Only those with the Master Gardener in residence will be safe. To burn, you have to be resolute in keeping Him out, refusing to allow Him any say in your garden. I cannot conceive of such suicidal stupidity.

But I have seen this parable apply to personal weeds too. It's easier to see in other people's gardens than in your own. Somebody in your church has a very obvious, flourishing weed, and you want to walk over there and yank it out. In Christian love, of course. If you give in to temptation, you are likely to lose the brother altogether. If you leave the gardening to Jesus and pay attention to what you love and admire about your brother, amazingly those are the blossoms that will grow, and you'll almost forget the weed. Later, you'll realize it's disappeared altogether!

Years ago, I heard a man telling of his conversion. He described how in the first flush of new love for God he read his Bible by the hour, flicking away the cigarette ashes and keeping his mind clear by frequent recourse to the beer bottle at his side. "Now I've learned how much health principles have to do with my ability to clearly follow God," he said. "But I am grateful to God that He loves sinners enough to start patiently weeding! I am grateful for His patience, as He taught me, in His own order and in His own time, all the things He wanted me to know. Most of all, I am grateful that no well-meaning brother shoved me right off the track by telling me all the things I had to do and stop doing, right now!"

I'm grateful too. This man was now a wonderful evangelist, and he reached young people in an incredible way. Like Peter, he still retained bruises from his own falls, and wasn't about to push anyone else down.

The moral of the story: Pull no weed before God's time. Reckon and count and consider them all dead. If they keep coming back (and they will) keep right on faithfully (with gritted teeth, if necessary) considering them *dead*. Cultivate and train the virtues, and leave the weeds to God. Here is what John the Baptist said would happen after your baptism: " 'I baptize you with water for repentance, but He who is coming after me is mightier than I . . . ; He Himself will baptize you with the Holy Spirit and fire. And His winnowing fork is in His hand, and He will thoroughly clear His threshing floor; and He will gather His wheat into the barn, but He will burn up the chaff with unquenchable fire' " (Matthew 3:11, 12). Amen! Hallelujah! So long, weeds! Even their ashes will enrich my garden!

Yes, I know, this text also means people and refers to the end of the age. But until then, there's still hope. " 'You were like a firebrand snatched from a blaze,' ... declares the Lord" (Amos 4:11). Weak and faulty as we are, even we can be snatched from the blaze and can snatch others from it, too. Jude, Jesus' brother, (who took a while coming to belief himself) ends his beautiful little letter this way:

> But you, beloved, building yourselves up on your most holy faith; praying in the Holy Spirit; keep yourselves in the love of God, waiting anxiously for the mercy of our Lord Jesus Christ to eternal life. And have mercy on some, who are doubting; save others, snatching them out of the fire; and on some have mercy with fear, hating even the garment polluted by the flesh. Now to Him who is able to keep you from stumbling, and to make you stand in the presence of His glory blameless with great joy, to the only God our Savior, through Jesus Christ our Lord, be glory, majesty, dominion and authority, before all time and now and forever. Amen (Jude 20-25).

He means be careful, because if people are polluted with pride, *you* can get a rash. But never leave someone else in a flaming garden if the Gardener asks you to help Him pull her out. Just make sure you leave the weeding, and all the rest of her gardening as well, to Him.

DIG DEEPER

When Jesus has taken your weaknesses and "composted" them into strengths, how has He used them to help and nurture others?

Are there some useful and positive characteristics in your life that are out of control? Pray that God will teach you when and how to say No, whether to yourself or to others. For help, look at Luke 4:16-43, a story of when Jesus, after a long day, actually said No. Do you think it was easy for Him? How and where did He find the strength, according to the story?

Write in your own words how you understand the difference between the sinful nature and sins as actions.

Spend some serious time in prayer asking God to show you if there is any poisonous pride in you. Give Him total permission to take away every bit of it. Keep your eyes on Him and on the virtues He is growing in you, thanking Him always for His grace. That way, you will be in no danger of either side of pride—self-righteousness and conceit or false humility and a "martyr" mentality.

How can you have mercy on other sinners, as well as yourself, leaving the weeding to God, without being "easy on sin"?

Snapshots From My Garden

She had learned more about weeding than she ever thought there was to know. She was also almost as tired as she used to be when the gardening first began. Some places were now totally weed free, the weeds having been picked and pulled by hand. Others were hoed and raked and had only a few weeds. Others, especially in grain patches, the Gardener had told her to leave until harvest. The plants were too close together. The roots were mingled, and if they pulled up the weeds, they would lose the grains as well.

"Where did the weeds come from?" she asked Him wearily.

"An enemy planted them," He answered, and His face looked grim. She had never seen Him look so grim. It made her shiver.

In the weeding, she had also noticed, being closer to the plants than she had been for a while, that some of them had spots and holes, weak stems, or hosts of worms. From a distance, from the arbor by the gate, for instance, the garden had looked so beautiful. It was depressing to discover that it wasn't as healthy and lush as she had thought.

She cried over a rose that had been perfect, but was now filled with beetles and holes. "What can we do?" she wailed.

"Lots of things," said the Gardener, no more at a loss than He ever was.

And so began a new stage of her learning. She made traps and sprays, picked bugs and worms, and pruned and burned damaged foliage and blossoms. But just when she began to be disheartened by the whole experience and wonder if she really liked gardening at all, she came across the Gardener, hovering over a delicate bloom and smiling.

"Come and see," He said.

"I'm busy," she demurred, but then recalled herself and came to admire the flower.

"You're obsessing again," He observed.

She was not the same person she once had been. Instead of whining and defending, she grinned. "Who, me?"

"Come and swing with Me."

She dropped her gloves and sprays and went. In their swing, swaying gently, the Gardener said, "Listen carefully. I am going to tell you the absolutely very best defense against every bug and pest and disease in the world."

She perked up. "Now? After all this work? Now You're going to tell me the secret?"

"Now that you've known the work, you'll take Me seriously."

"OK. What is it?"

"Keep a healthy garden."

She waited. He pushed the swing gently with His foot. That appeared to be the sum total of His gem of wisdom for the day.

"What?"

"Keep a healthy garden. Do you remember how I've taught you to do that?"

"Well, let's see. You plow, then disk . . ."

"No, no," He interrupted. "You've missed the first part."

"Oh, right. I sit with You in the swing, rain or shine." He smiled, so she went on. "I drink from the spring all day, every day. I do deep breathing exercises in the fresh air. Then, You and I together plow and disk and cultivate, plan and plant, weed and hoe, feed and compost and mulch and water . . . um . . . have I left out anything?"

"In short, you spend your time and energy and love on the good plants—the beautiful plants—the plants you want. They will grow strong and able to withstand anything life throws at them."

She thought about it. "And I've been spending my time on pests and weeds and diseases, haven't I?" He didn't have to answer. She knew she had. "So what will we do today?" she asked.

"Let's plan a creature garden."

"A what?"

"A creature garden. A garden that attracts butterflies, bees, ladybugs, robins, toads, and other beneficial creatures. Then they'll do some of the work for us."

She jumped up. "How do we begin?"

CHAPTER 12

Pests and Diseases: Spiritual Sprays for Sickly Souls

I have been trying to grow a dwarf fruit orchard for some time now, with limited success. With very limited success! My first mistake was planting it where a tangle of wild brambles and berries used to be. So now I continually fight brambles, which are pretty much un-killable, and where I succeed in beating them back, burdock takes over. On top of that, I don't spray. I keep on believing, with gritted teeth, that there must be a way to grow my food, even my fruit, without poisons. Then there's my decidedly inexpert pruning.

Occasionally I get an apple or pear or two. The cherries gave up the ghost long ago. But the peach tree, by last year, was looking pretty good. It had even lived through the incredible invasion of the dreaded "seventeen-year locusts" and the terrible, harsh pruning they necessitated. (What do I know? Maybe it needed that awful pruning!)

Anyway, when spring came, the peach tree bloomed like a pink cloud. I thought, "This year for sure . . . !" Hundreds of baby peaches appeared in due course. Eagerly, hopefully, I watched them grow. About halfway to maturity, they all rotted and fell off.

I don't know yet whether it was a pest or a disease. I do know I'm starting a new orchard this year, in a better location, and I'm putting into practice all the things I've learned by hard experience, including organic sprays of soaps, oils, and other harmless or fairly harmless compounds. But I know that even without sprays, my trees will do better than they have before. Because they will be growing in a place that meets their needs, so that they can be healthy and strong, and better able to fight off anything poor, sick, aging Mother Nature may throw at them.

That's something I've finally learned in my own life too. When I live in a healthy place, in a healthy way, I am stronger. When I see to it that the needs of my body and spirit are met, they are better able to cope with the battles of life.

I may be stretching the garden analogy a little far in this chapter. Maybe, spiritually speaking, weeds, pests, and diseases are all the same thing—inroads of sin. Certainly you'll recognize some of the suggested antidotes as items we've examined before. But the only point of an analogy is to give humans a mental picture that makes spiritual concepts easier to grasp and put into practice. And different pictures work for different people, or even for the same person in different circumstances. So for purposes of definition, let's say that spiritual "diseases" come from the inside and spiritual "pests" come from the outside. In this chapter, we'll examine some common pests and diseases of the spiritual garden, and some effective antidotes against them.

GUILT

The details in the following story have been changed. An achingly large number of people will still recognize themselves in it.

Marcel was in the Vietnam War. He scoffs when people remind him it was only a "conflict." "I was there," he'll tell you grimly. "It was war." He did his duty. He went, when his friends were protesting and burning their draft cards. He felt patriotic and noble about it at the time. And scared, of course. As well as a boy can be, Marcel was prepared for the grim horrors of shooting and being shot. He was even prepared for the possibility of being taken prisoner, possibly tortured. War, he knew, is hell.

But Marcel was not prepared for the realities of Vietnam. When he came back, he was so different it was as if he really had not come back at all. His family thought he had died in the inferno and someone else had come back in his body. They weren't far wrong. He never told anyone about the shadows that now haunted him. He refused to talk about the war at all, saying it was over, and he didn't want to think about it. But he never entered another church. Nothing anyone could say or do seemed to make the slightest impact. Marcel withdrew into his shell and refused to come out.

A very young, inexperienced pastor came to town. He felt called by God to visit Marcel, but also terrified of the idea. What on earth could he say to this torn and trampled shadow of a man? He had never been to war. And Marcel never talked to anybody. He certainly would not talk to Pastor Tom. But God kept calling, so Pastor Tom went. And went again. One day, Marcel started to talk. Pastor Tom listened and prayed and tried desperately not to betray his sick horror.

"So I shot them," Marcel finished dully. "I was ordered to, and I did. I see them explode again every night in my dreams. Everybody thinks I've lost my faith, but they're wrong. I believe in God. And I know He could never forgive a man who shot children—babies!—just because he was told to." He sat in silence for a minute. "It's OK, pastor. You can go now. You've done your duty."

Pastor Tom didn't move. He had never felt so young and inadequate. Nothing in his life connected with anything in Marcel's life. But young or not, there was one thing he knew. So he said it. "God forgives everything. Everything, Marcel. He knows. He is the only One who knows exactly what you did and why and how you feel about it. He's seen every dream and heard every scream. And Marcel . . ." Tom slipped to his knees in front of Marcel and grabbed his hanging head in shaking hands. "God has those children safe! He will bring them back to life when He comes. You know He will. Marcel!" He shook the head in his hands, trying to find some sign of life. "God loves you! He died for you! Your sins are forgiven!"

Not knowing what else to do, Tom kept repeating himself and praying and holding on to Marcel. And the dam broke. Marcel fell half onto the floor and half into Tom's arms and cried until he was sick.

Guilt, one of the most insidious and deadly diseases of the soul because it seems so right and so righteous, had almost killed Marcel. Forgiveness is the only antidote for guilt, and it's hard to swallow. A person in the final stages of guilt believes that if he accepts forgiveness, he's saying that what he did is OK. If he stops feeling the anguish, it will mean he has excused himself. We must come to understand clearly that forgiveness is necessary only when there is no excuse! If there is an excuse for what you did, you say, "Oops! I'm sorry!" The person on whose toe you stepped says, "Oh, that's OK." No forgiveness is necessary. It is only when what you did was wrong, was sin, was part of what killed God, and there is no excuse for it—that you need forgiveness! Jesus bought that forgiveness at a terrible price we do not begin to understand and probably never will understand. Take it. Let it soak deep into the roots of your life, and the healing will begin. The branches will lift toward the sun, and leaves will grow again. God promises it, and your Father never lies. I don't care what you did or how terrible it was. God is holding out forgiveness to you. Accept it, and live.

FEAR

I recognize this ugly disease all too well. I let it live and grow at the roots of my heart, only half recognizing it. One day, meditating in my inner garden, I begged the Master Gardener to show me what was wrong with my sickly, ailing spiritual life. He took me by the hand and led me to the base of the tree, which, in my mind, represents my life. He pulled back some weeds and showed me something that shocked me. There, coiled around the roots of my tree, was a huge, loathsome snake, sucking the life out of the roots. I recoiled in horror.

"It's Fear," said Jesus. "You've let it grow until it's almost killed you. Please let Me get rid of it."

Of course I said Yes. But I recognized an irrational battle too. If I let go of fear, it meant that I had to accept cheerfully anything that might happen to me as being part of God's overall plan for my life. It meant bad things might happen. I don't know how I thought fear would help—keep me prepared at least, I guess. I can tell you fear never stopped anything bad from happening to me! But it felt as if giving up fear would make scary things more likely to happen to me. And I wouldn't even be allowed to dread them. Worse, I would have to welcome them. Because the antidote to fear is trust, and trust means I really believe, in the minutes of everyday life, not just during the sermon, that God is holding me every second and working out His perfect plan for me.

Then there was Elizabeth, nearly lost in bitterness and hatred. She had every reason—every right!—to feel bitter and hateful toward the person who had wantonly hurt her. When she nourished the hatred, it felt as if she were paying back the other person. Of course, in her more rational moments, she knew that wasn't true. She was hurting no one but herself. In fact, the best description of bitterness I ever heard was: "Holding on to bitterness is like drinking poison and waiting for the other guy to die!"

However, giving forgiveness is as hard as accepting it. If you forgive, it feels as if you're saying what the other person did was OK. Read it again. It's only when there is no excuse that you need forgiveness.

Marcel, Elizabeth, and I could all tell you that letting Jesus administer the antidote to our guilt, shame, fear, and hate does not mean there is instant, full health. We didn't get sick in a minute, and we won't get well in a minute. He pours on the forgiveness, love, and care, and we spend hours and weeks and years digging it into the soil of our hearts, making it a part of us until we couldn't give it up if we tried. We spend our time paying attention to the things we do want, leaning on the forgiveness, giving it out as freely as it was given to us, loving and trusting and singing while we work. And we grow green and strong and healthy, until one day the fruit that we bear feeds another soul fainting under the same spiritual disease we once had. That's the true circle of life.

Oh, by the way, you can get an instant cure, if at the very first sign of trouble, you rush to the Master Gardener and get a large dose of the antidote right away. Disease will never get a foothold, and your health will continue unabated. Amazing, isn't He?

There are many more of these spiritual diseases—discouragement, irritability, worry, impatience, an unloving attitude. The list seems nearly endless. The antidotes are already growing in us—love, joy, peace, patience . . . If God is in us, the cure is in us. The question is: To which are we paying attention? Are we worrying about our bad habit of worrying? Or are we practicing peace in every situation? What you spend time cultivating will grow. It's the rule of gardening. Yes, the enemy is still there, and he's still planting tares and snickering. Ignore him and stick with the Gardener, and do everything He tells you to do.

What about pests? Pests fly in from outside, and there's not a thing you can do to prevent them. My mother used to say, "You can't stop the birds from flying over your head, but you can prevent them from building nests in your hair!" Let's look at some common pests that nibble at the spiritual life.

TEMPTATIONS

Probably the single most ubiquitous and unavoidable pest in the spiritual world is the common, garden-variety temptation. They can attack in swarms like gnats, hovering around your head until you want to scream, or individually, like one fat, persistent, maddening blue-bottle. I'm not sure which is worse. But it's important to know that, like flies, they can't really hurt your garden unless you give them something to eat. If they start feeding and multiplying, you're in trouble, because they carry disease, among other things.

There are only two defenses against these irritating creatures—prayer and the Word of God. As soon as you spot incoming temptations, run, do not walk, to the Gardener. He'll give you ammunition that works better than any earthly bug spray. However, it's far better to lay out repellents in advance.

Recently, I've tried something that works so well that it's a tribute to the strength and persistence of fallen human nature that I still haven't learned to use it always. In the morning, during my early devotional time, I find promises that I know will protect me against temptations that I am aware of in advance. In other words, if I have a task to do that

I'm dreading, and I know perfectly well that I will be strongly tempted to avoid it (again), I'll find a promise such as, "The hand of the diligent will rule, but the slack hand will be put to forced labor" (Proverbs 12:24). If I can find several verses like this, I consciously claim them from God, write them on cards, and actually carry them in my pocket, practicing and learning them throughout the day. When temptation comes, I am already armed and dangerous. But would you believe, just having these Bible promises ready often seems to act as an actual repellent? That is, temptation either doesn't come at all, or I hardly notice it when it does!

Of course, temptations often come as a surprise that you couldn't have been ready for in advance. So you stock up on all the promises you can and practice being consciously aware of Jesus' presence at your side. Warning: the cards are not magic. The verses are not magic. The Bible itself is not magic. It is the power of God Himself you must depend on; without Him, the Bible is just ink on paper. If you start relying on certain words of Scripture as if they were some runic spell, you will poison yourself with your own bug spray. Don't forget: He's the Gardener; you're just the caretaker.

What are some other pests that come from outside yourself?

CRITICISM

Other people will come and look over your garden walls and offer you all kinds of free advice. Some will be great, some fairly harmless, and some simply negative and hurtful. It's enough to make you throw in the trowel and retire under the branches of your tree where no one can see you. What can you do when people throw insults at you? Throw them back? Try to pretend they didn't hurt you or that you don't even notice them?

Here's an idea. When someone throws rotten fruit at you, the first thing to do—as always—is to call on the Gardener. Then, together, hold your nose, put on gloves, and pick through it to see if there are any seeds of truth there. Uncomfortably often, you will find some. If you find any, plant them! Compost the rest, and it will eventually enrich you, despite the intentions of the fruit-thrower. And if there are no good seeds to be found, compost it all! Your criticizer's loss is your gain.

When I was young, I found out to my intense dismay that some people thought I was "stuck up." I was horrified. I had a lot of faults, but that was the last one I would ever have expected to be accused of. First, as was my habit, I brooded over the comments and cried. I knew perfectly well they were not true. In fact, I was actually very insecure, the exact opposite of a conceited attitude that could be considered "stuck up." Jesus showed me some things I could do then to show love and help change people's ideas of me.

He must have also planted some seeds. Because over the years, as I grew in understanding and in my own confidence and security, I finally realized that hidden in those hurtful criticisms, there really were seeds of truth! My very insecurity caused me to tend to withdraw into myself because I was afraid people wouldn't like me or I would be hurt. This is what caused the attitude that some people saw as standoffish and cold. If they had only known that inside I was longing to be liked and to make friends as easily as other people seemed to. I have come to see that I was hiding out, in effect saying, "Inside here, I'm a really nice person, but you're never going to know that, because I suspect you are a mean person who would hurt me. So I have to protect myself from you." Well, what is that if not a twisted sort of pride? It certainly wasn't con-scious or intentional, and I didn't think I was proud since we usually think of pride as a deliberate sort of holding up one's nose at the rest of humanity. Not only did Jesus plant those seeds and grow them into a new understanding but He composted the rest of the hurtfulness, and now I am able to see through others' standoffishness to the hurt and fear underneath. The seed from that old rotten fruit that hurt and em-barrassed me is alive and well and bearing fresh fruit of its own today.

Isn't the Gardener amazing?

UNKINDNESS

Sometimes criticism grows to deliberate unkindness. Sometimes you're not paranoid; someone really is out to get you! Now what? Well, the first antidote to unkindness is kindness. You can find prom-ises for this in the Sermon on the Mount and in Paul's and Peter's letters to the young church. You and God have been cultivating kindness anyway, and this is your opportunity to put it to the test. Often, by the grace of God, simple kindness will heal the breach. Invite the boys who keep breaking branches in your orchard and stealing apples over to your house and bake apple crisp for them; they may well be so ashamed that they never bother your orchard again. Give up your church office to the person who has been loudly criticizing your efforts; later she may come and apologize and ask you to help her in her work.

Of course, you should always ask Jesus what to do. He is the only One who knows just what to do in every instance. Don't even follow the above examples without asking Him first. And some people will be unkind no matter what. There will be times when Jesus will tell you that all you can do is pray and avoid the person who wants to hurt you. You can keep loving that person, but you may have to do it from a safe distance.

God says to let our enemy slap the other cheek and to go the second mile with him or her, but He also says to love others as you love yourself. Self-respect is important, and it's also catching. It is rarely a loving or kind thing to do to let someone continue actions that are harming his soul much more than they are harming your body and/or spirit. Do not stick around to be someone's whipping post. But never stop praying. He is not the Master Gardener for nothing, and He has shown that He can cut down whole trees and still redeem the garden.

BUSYNESS

A dangerous critter, busyness will quickly bring a garden to its knees. It will revert with shocking speed back to the jungle or swamp it once was, if neglected. If you notice this pest, go immediately back to the beginning and start spending time sitting with the Gardener in the sun, dancing with Him in the rain, breathing in the Holy Spirit. Let Him tell you what your priorities are to be and whether something should be deleted from your life. There's nothing you can gain that will make up for the loss of your soul's garden.

WRONG TEACHINGS

This is a serious pest and can wreak havoc in a garden. Not everything that looks like a beneficial insect is one. This problem is especially prevalent in new gardens, but can happen to anybody sometime. Someone you trust teaches you falsehood in the place of truth. The worst thing about this is that it is self-perpetuating. One person learns a falsehood and accepts it as truth; teaches it to others, who share it . . . and off we go. There are a lot of false doctrines out there, and they all got their start just this way.

There's only one defense against this destructive pest. You must know your Bible for yourself. Study it alone, with no one but the Gardener. You can use concordances to help you find things, but even commentaries and Bible study aids were all written by human beings, and some of them are flat-out wrong. You won't know what to believe until you know your own Bible. Then you'll be able to gain from the insights of other caretakers. God promised you would hear His voice and that His Spirit would lead you into all truth. It's up to you to decide if that's what you really want. He also talks a lot about His people clinging to falsehood because it's what they're used to and because it's hard to give up a cherished belief. Here are some hard questions for you (and me) to ponder: Do we worship and adore God, or our ideas about God? Are we willing to have our ideas changed if they need to be? How will we know if they need changing unless we dig in the Scriptures for ourselves?

ANOTHER IMPORTANT WARNING

You can get so caught up looking for and eradicating pests that you can't enjoy the garden. Another insidious pest, almost the Japanese beetle of the spiritual world, is the thoughts that fly in concerning past sins. Or present or future ones, for that matter.

Even though I know I'm forgiven, I still feel so bad . . .

Today's going to be busy. I'll never get everything done, so I might as well just give up . . .

I just can't help it; if I see her I'm going to lose my temper . . .

Stop. Just close your eyes, turn away, and look at what you do want. Open your eyes to the Master Gardener, arm yourself with His Word, busy yourself cultivating the virtues He has planted in you, listen to His voice, breathe in His Spirit, and breathe out praise. "I am confident of this very thing, that He who began a good work in you will perfect it until the day of Christ Jesus.... And this I pray, that your love may abound still more and more in real knowledge and all discernment, so that you may approve the things that are excellent, in order to be sincere and blameless until the day of Christ; having been filled with the fruit of righteousness which comes through Jesus Christ, to the glory and praise of God" (Philippians 1:6-11).

DIG DEEPER

Guilt, fear, worry, insecurity, hatred, bitterness—are inner diseases such as these poisoning your soul? In each case, the antidote is the opposite of the disease. In other words, the antidote to worry is trust, the antidote to discouragement is faith, etc. Write down any diseases that have caused you trouble and determine what the antidotes are. Then take the disease to God and ask for a healthy dose of the antidote. From that moment on, with all the determination of which you are capable (and you will grow more and more capable), concentrate all your thought on Jesus as the Source of that antidote. Trust Him for it and believe it is yours. For example, don't pray "Help me not to be fearful and agitated." Pray, "Thank You for promising that I can be filled with peace." If He said He'd give you peace, you are calling Him a liar if you don't really believe and claim that you are now a peaceful person. I know it feels like a lie to say, "I love Jane," when you've felt nothing but hate for her for years. But it's not a lie if you've accepted God's love for Jane as your own. It's a statement of faith. Do this and live. (And call the Doctor every morning!)

What are some of the "pests" that bother you on a regular basis? Ask God how to deal with them, and do what He tells you.

Write about a time when a criticism someone threw at you had seeds of truth in it, and what has grown from that painful experience.

Snapshots From My Garden

In all her orgy of weeding, there was one corner she hadn't touched. A jungle of thorny briars thrived there, spreading almost fast enough to watch and poking their scratchy fingers into everything that came near. They had made her bleed more than once, and even reached their thorns over the wall and scratched others who visited. She was powerless to do anything about them, and when she asked the Gardener He said to leave them be for now. It seemed strange. Maybe it was like the weeds whose roots were tangled with the grain, which were to be left until harvest.

But one day, He brought pruning shears, jackets, and heavy gloves and told her that today was the day they would deal with the briar patch. Interested, but nervous, she followed Him to the area in question. He stood back and looked at the thicket of prickly vines from several different angles as if studying it.

"See?" He pointed. "There, and there. Those are the strongest. We'll save them and dig out all these weaker ones."

"Save them! Why?"

He smiled. "They may seem worthless to you, but all they need is some control to be very good, productive plants."

She was amazed. She had thought they all must be destroyed. As she watched, He certainly was ruthless about those He had decided had to go. He showed her how to chop back the branches and then dig out the knotted root ball. Together they worked until they were sweaty and scratched, despite their protective clothing. They accumulated a large pile to be burned. The Gardener told her they would put the cooled ashes on the compost pile.

Then He stood back again, and surveyed the survivors, now standing alone in cleared patches. "Now we have to prune the ones we have left."

This she was allowed only to watch. He explained each cut, and when He was finished, the plants looked much neater, with only a few strong limbs each, no weak or crossing branches, and all open to the sunlight. This time He had accumulated two piles. One was to be burned. The other, to her surprise, they transplanted by sticking the stems into the ground in a neat row, in a patch of prepared ground near the east wall where they would receive abundant sunlight and warmth. "We'll water and feed these carefully," He told her. "By next year they'll be as big and strong as their parents."

She was still mystified as to their purpose, but she had learned to trust Him and wait.

Next they went to the young fruit trees nearby, planted right against the wall (too close, she had always privately thought). They took off their hot gloves and jackets, and the Gardener explained that these fruit trees were to be espaliered. She had no idea what that meant, but again, waited to see.

The Gardener took His pruning shears and began to snip off most of the young branches. She couldn't help wincing. These trees were growing so well! They had put out strong limbs and leaves, and now He was cutting them off! She smothered a protest. Did she trust Him or didn't she?

The Gardener had placed hooks in the wall at each end of the row. Several lengths of strong cord crossed behind the trees, stretching from hook to hook. When He had only a few branches on each little tree, He carefully tied these branches horizontally along the cords. When He was finished, the Gardener stood back and looked with satisfaction at His handiwork. The row of trees looked like a work of art, a pattern of lace against the jeweled, lapis lazuli wall.

"You'll see," He assured her. "These trees will produce the largest, most perfect fruit you've ever eaten!"

She gathered up the branches. "I hope so. It just seems so sad to cut off good growth! I understand about cutting off dead and diseased wood, but doesn't it hurt the trees to cut off good wood they've worked hard to grow?"

"Yes, but not for long. If they could talk, they would tell you it was worth it in the end. Wait and see. Now, we have one more job today."

He led her to the rose garden where some wild roses He had planted were flourishing. To her dismay, He cut off their entire tops, and with a very sharp knife, sliced straight cuts down into the top of the stump. While her mouth was still open in a gasp, He took cuttings of some tea roses they had been pampering and inserted them into the cut stumps. Then He bound the joints together and coated them with a warm wax mixture from a small pot. Carefully inspecting the results, He said that they would keep a close watch on these plants, as well.

She couldn't keep silent. "What are You doing?"

"It's called 'grafting.' The tea roses will now have the strength of the wild roses and will be able to concentrate on blooming, instead of struggling through cold or storms."

"But the wild roses . . . !"

"They'll produce blooms they never could have produced before!"

He grinned at her confused face and repeated His motto: "Wait and see!"

She took His hand and smiled back. "I'm waiting."

CHAPTER 13

Pruning, Staking, and Grafting: Here a Snip, There a Stake, All Tied Up in Love

As we grow in the Lord, we become more willing to bear His cutting out the dead and diseased parts of ourselves. Even though it is painful at the time, we recognize that it is necessary. In fact, as we mature, we begin to truly desire God to remove all that keeps us apart from Him or that interferes with our relationship. We begin to discover—not because the pastor, or even the Bible, says so, but through personal experience—that those things He removes aren't even parts of our *real* selves, the perfect disciples God plans us to be. They feel like it when they're cut off, but after they're gone, we are more ourselves than we have ever been. It's a wonderfully freeing realization!

Then He starts cutting into the "good stuff."

Luigi turned his restaurant into an inner-city mission. People came to him at all hours of the day and night, not just for physical food, but for spiritual food. Everybody knew you could go to Luigi for anything—anything at all. He was almost like having Jesus around in the flesh!

Then financial problems began, and Luigi was faced with the fear that he would have to close down. He prayed desperately, and as he did so he realized, to his dismay, that God was actually calling him to close the mission and move. "Are You sure, Lord? What about these people? Am I to just abandon them? Wasn't this Your idea in the first place? Why are You taking away from me the one thing I love most?" Luigi was mature enough as a Christian to know God had a plan and that the people he worried about were God's children, not his. But it hurt.

Sandra was given the ministry of helping others. She made things for people, gave gifts, offered hospitality. Over the years, she grew to be truly excellent at what she did. Hundreds, maybe even thousands, of people were deeply affected by her life. Then she was in a frightful accident. She lost the use of her body and had to enter a nursing home. She thought she could handle that if only she could use her hands. If only she could still make things for people, even in the nursing home. She couldn't even speak well. "Why, God?" she wept. "Didn't You give me my ministry? Wasn't it Your idea? And if it's over, then why can't I just die? Is there still any use for me?"

In Isaiah, Jesus says that because His beloved vineyard was rebellious and refused to cooperate with Him, it will be laid waste. " 'It will not be pruned or hoed, but briars and thorns will come up' " (Isaiah 5:6). In other words, being pruned is part of His care, and not being pruned is part of being laid waste. That's too bad, according to my human feelings. I would rather not be pruned. But then I look at John 15:1, 2. " 'I am the true vine, and My Father is the vinedresser. Every branch in Me that does not bear fruit, He takes away; and every branch that bears fruit, He prunes it, *that it may bear more fruit*' " (emphasis supplied). Ah! In that case, "Prune me, Lord. I want to bear all the fruit I can for You."

Luigi submitted cheerfully to God's leading and is now a teacher at a culinary institute. People come from several countries to learn from him. He will not know until he reaches heaven how many thousands of people are now touched by the love demonstrated in mission restaurants all over the world, whose owners or managers learned from Luigi's experienced methods.

Sandra gave herself up to God's hands and is beloved by the whole nursing home staff and residents because of the aroma of godliness that hovers around her. With very few words, just her sweet smile and loving patience, she has been instrumental in the saving of several souls that had been so hardened by their constant exposure to suffering that they had come to believe God didn't exist or didn't care. Sandra doesn't even know the miracles God is working through her. She only knows her inner devotional life is richer than it ever was in her busy days.

Pruning isn't comfortable, but God is an expert. We can trust Him not to cut away anything necessary. There's another way He uses pruning too. He can take those shears and turn something we thought was all bad, or at least useless, into something beautiful and productive.

I'm thinking specifically of anger. We are so often taught that anger is sinful. Women, especially, are trained never to show anger. "Christian ladies don't even feel anger, and if they do, they certainly do not allow it to appear!" I used to do my desperate best to live by that adage. The problem was, the feelings *were* there! I struggled to deny them, but they grew and spread until my heart was a jungle of scratchy, bleeding pain. And then those feelings burst out all over everybody, usually at the worst possible time, and on the people I loved the most. I prayed, but unknowingly I was praying the wrong prayer. I wanted God to take away all my anger, and He wouldn't do it. How was I to know He actually *wanted* some of that awful stuff?

He began to send people—pastors, counselors, friends—who told me emotions are just emotions. Like pimples, everybody has them. They come and go, but they are neither good nor bad of themselves. The question is: How do we use them? These counselors pointed out that Paul said, "Be angry, and yet do not sin" (Ephesians 4:26).

"Fine," I replied. "I accept that. How *do* I use them?"

I took a short course on anger management. I read a lot. I prayed more. I began to cautiously practice. Sometimes successfully. One of the most valuable things that happened was the story I told in chapter 6 of this book, of my visit to the throne room of God, when I gave Him my anger and He transformed it into something beautiful, which He said I could learn to use for Him. I have to say, those moments when I can see anger as having any beauty are incredibly rare, but I'm learning to use it sometimes.

Little by little, inside my heart, God has been pruning and transplanting and bringing the jungle under control. But if you have, in your real garden, any of what are fondly known as bramble fruits, you know you have to stay on top of those things! They can get out of control and take over the landscape again in no time at all. Luckily, I have a Master Gardener who is an expert at what He does.

Often, after pruning, there is staking to be done. Peter, who knew from personal experience exactly what he was talking about, puts it this way: "After you have suffered for a little while, the God of all grace, who called you to His eternal glory in Christ, will Himself perfect, confirm, strengthen and establish you" (1 Peter 5:10). He adds, "To Him be dominion forever and ever. Amen" (verse 11). I echo heartily, Amen!

The Bible says that our strength is God's arm. Speaking of His servant David, and by extension, of all His servants, God says, " 'With whom My hand will be established; My arm also will strengthen him' " (Psalm 89:21). Isaiah 41:10 is one of my favorite promises. " ' "I will strengthen you, surely I will help you, surely I will uphold you with My righteous right hand." ' " How exactly does that happen? Through God on earth, the Holy Spirit.

Jesus made it clear in His final discourse to His disciples, found in John 13 through 17, that the Holy Spirit would now be His representative on earth, and that through the Spirit's constant presence with us, we could actually be closer to God than the disciples were, who had only a physical Jesus who could be in only one place at a time. You don't have to go out in the morning and look for the Spirit because He has gone away somewhere to pray. He is in unbroken communion with the Father and the Son, and, if you let Him, with you, too. So read the following verses, thoughtfully, with the clear understanding that they are meant to be a conscious reality in your daily life. He is your stake, if you will, and you can live and move and have your being tied close to His side, strengthened in Him by the bonds of love, trust, and surrender.

"That He would grant you, according to the riches of His glory, to be *strengthened* with power through His Spirit in the inner man; so that Christ may dwell in your hearts through faith; and that you, [may be] *rooted and grounded* in love" (Ephesians 3:16, 17, emphasis supplied).

"That you may . . . please Him in all respects, *bearing fruit* in every good work and increasing in the knowledge of God; *strengthened with all power,* according to His glorious might, for the attaining of all stead-fastness and patience" (Colossians 1:10, 11, emphasis supplied).

"I can do all things through Him who *strengthens* me" (Philippians 4:13, emphasis supplied).

Notice that the strength that is available to you is measured according to God's glorious might and power. I don't think this stake will weaken and fall over or ever be unable to support you. But the ties are love. They are God's unlimited love for you, but they are also your choice of loving Him. You can let those rot and fall away. Please don't.

In a small way, we can also be stakes for one another. Our support is much weaker and more precarious than God's, but we can sometimes hold each other up long enough to get each other tied to the Spirit. The Bible contains quite a few admonitions to provide this kind of support for those who need it. "We urge you, brethren, admonish the unruly, encourage the fainthearted, help the weak, be patient with all men" (1 Thessalonians 5:14). " 'Help the weak and remember the words of the Lord Jesus, . . . "It is more blessed to give than to receive" ' " (Acts 20:35).

Sometimes we get confused, though, about what it really means to help the weak. Our churches are full of what we have come to call "care-takers" or "codependents," people who allow others to depend on them rather than on God, and who find their own self-worth in being needed by these weak ones. Remember that to stake a plant means to tie a vine or young tree to a pole stronger than itself so that it can grow. Care must be taken to see to it that the plant does not grow into its ties or its stake. This can happen, and always causes damage. I've seen it happen in spiritual realities, too, when the stake is a person instead of God. No human is innately stronger than any other, and no human depending too closely on another will ever grow to full potential. The only reason for the differentiation of "weaker" and "stronger" Christians is to define those who, through time and experience, have learned to remain closely tied to the Spirit, and those who are just learning or whose connection to the Spirit is only intermittent.

In Isaiah 35:3, 4 we learn more specifically *how* we are to help and support each other. This passage is in the context of great trial and tumult. In fact, it's speaking of the "day of the Lord"—everything looks terrifying, and all seems lost. The "strongest" of us come to times like that and need encouragement from each other. The Master Gardener uses us as temporary stakes in many situations. He asks us to "encourage the exhausted, and strengthen the feeble" (verse 3). But we are not to encourage the fainting one to lean on *us*. Verse 4: "Say to those with anxious heart, 'Take courage, fear not. Behold, your God will come with vengeance; the recompense of God will come, [in your terror it may seem He is out to get you] but *He will save you*' " (emphasis supplied).

When we use our God-given gifts of encouragement and help and kindness to help others retie their bonds of love and trust to the only One who can safely hold them up, we are doubly blessed ourselves. David learned "how blessed is he who considers the helpless; the Lord will deliver him in a day of trouble. The Lord will protect him, and keep him alive, and he shall be called blessed upon the earth" (Psalm 41:1, 2). Mothers and fathers who have carefully trained their children to grow out of dependence on them and into dependence on God can attest to this truth. Eventually, their children really do "rise up and bless [them]" (Proverbs 31:28).

That leaves one more gardening subject for this chapter, and that's the interesting subject of grafting. The Bible's only discourse on grafting is in Romans 11:17-24, and it is speaking of the grafting of the Gentiles to the "rich root of the olive tree." The Israelites believed this rich root was Israel, but Paul points out in this chapter that Israelites are only branches, not roots. They are not the source of nourishment. They can be cut off for unbelief. Then he warns the Gentiles, that they, too, are only branches and can still be cut off if they are arrogant toward the Israelites. He doesn't say so in so many words, but it is clear that the root is Jesus Himself. That is shown in other places, as well. Jesus says He is the Vine, and in several visions, olive trees or olive oil lamps represent the Spirit of God.

So we, whether Gentiles or Jews by birth, are all really grafted into Jesus. And in this life, I think it would be safe to say that all our virtues are grafted into us, too. We are given a new nature when we believe, but we will not own that new nature in its fullness until we are glorified at the coming of the Root and Vine and Gardener, our Lord Himself. Yet, by the miracle of grafting, we can bloom and bear fruit here as if we were glorified! A look at the practice of grafting will help to explain this.

Regarding grafting, *The Encyclopedia of Organic Gardening* (Rodale, 1978), p. 448, gives this thought-provoking definition: "A graft is a successful union of two diverse but related living plant pieces in such a way that the cambium or living conductor of nutrients and food of the lower piece or stock will connect with the cambium of the upper piece or scion. Then when the two match up, they can grow together and make one healthy living plant. Both the stock and scion are wounded before they are matched, and from the wounds of each a callus forms. The two calluses interweave in a successful graft even before the matching of cambiums takes place." It adds, "Grafting has been practiced for three thousand years, especially on fruit and olive trees, with many of the early grafts made to repair injuries from storm or other attacks on the trees."

Think of it! Step One: A Being impossibly diverse from us chooses to come down and be one of us so that He will be closely related. Step Two: Having grown strong, He is cut off completely. Step Three: We, who have been severely damaged by unimaginable storms in our habitat, are cut off our failing roots and grafted into His wounded stock. Step Four: The graft is bound, sealed, and tenderly cared for by the Vinedresser. Step Five: We grow strong and healthy and—listen! *Jesus can now bear His fruit only through us!*

There is one major difference between earthly and heavenly grafting. Here, the flowers and fruit are those of the scion, the top part of the graft. They gain strength and hardiness only from the rootstock. In God's plan, the fruit and flowers come only *through* the branches, directly from the rootstock, without which the scion could not bloom or bear fruit at all. So Jesus needs us, His branches, but the fruit we bear is all His.

To Him be all the honor and glory forever and ever, amen!

DIG DEEPER

List some of the dead and diseased things God has cut out of your life. How did it feel at the time? How do you feel about it now? Now list some good and positive things God has taken away or pruned. How do you feel about that? Are you learning to let Him have His way when to your human eyes He seems to be contradicting even Himself? Have you seen more fruit because of the pruning? What if you don't think there is more fruit?

Is anger under God's control in your life? What are some things you have learned about godly anger? How about some other qualities that can be both good and bad? Imagination? Guilty conscience? Appetites?

Check out the stakes and ties in your inner garden. Are they ties that hold you to God's love, or are they something else—duty, perhaps, or habit? Is the stake the Holy Spirit, or is it the church, a certain doctrine or a set of doctrines or even a person or group of people? What is your source of strength?

Is there someone you are leaning on in an unhealthy way, or allowing to lean on you? This can be very difficult to detect, so ask a pastor, Christian counselor, or trusted godly friend if you need to. Then decide together, prayerfully, what to do about it. It is often very dangerous to simply cut such ties all at once.

Spend some time meditating with God on the miracle of heavenly grafting, which allows you to actually become part of Jesus—"a partaker of divine nature"—and that makes it possible for Him to bear His fruit and flowers through you!

Snapshots From My Garden

The garden was a hum of noise and activity. People milled at the gate and wandered around outside the walls. There was laughter and singing in the air. She was surrounded by bright smiles and sparkling eyes. The harvest had begun!

Under the trellis at the gate, she and the Gardener had set up a table and loaded it with the fruits of their labors. Her friends and neighbors were filling their hands, their mouths, even their pockets, for sharing. She carried baskets of fruit and vegetables to hand out to those reaching over the walls. Flowers nodded over everything, in bowls on the table, in bouquets she passed over the wall, in corsages and chains in hair or around necks. To one and all, she repeated, over and over, "It's the Master Gardener who has done all this. That One—see, over there, with the beautiful eyes and the smile like sunshine? He will do the same in your garden. Please, talk to Him and ask Him in."

She felt satisfaction in seeing the people's immediate needs met by her fruit and vegetables, happiness when she saw their eyes lit up by her flowers. But nothing compared with the joy she felt when she saw some of them in earnest conversation with her Gardener. She knew some of these people lived in deserts, swamps, or hovels much like the one she could barely remember. If only there were words that could really show them the transformation, the joy and contentment and deep, abiding peace that was her life now! Some of them remembered her from before and watched her in awe and amazement. But the best she could do was to keep saying, "That One—the One everyone is flocking to like a magnet—see? Go to Him! Talk to Him! No job is too big or too hard for Him, I promise!"

By the end of the day, she was exhausted as she had never been from digging, hoeing, or weeding. The crowd had gone. She and the Gardener sat in the swing, her head limp on His shoulder, His toe moving the swing slowly to and fro. She felt an aura of joy radiating from Him that surpassed her own.

"It's a garden!" she said after a while.

His chuckle rumbled under her ear. "Yes, it is."

"I wondered, sometimes, if it ever would be."

"I know."

"Thank You so much! It was worth all the hard work!"

Another chuckle. "Oh, My child, the work has barely begun!"

She lifted her head.

"Tomorrow, we'll dig up another section, over by the northwest corner."

He didn't say what it was for. She put her head back down on His shoulder. "All right. Tomorrow." And she fell asleep.

The Gardener rocked gently in the moonlight, His face lifted to the sky, eyes reflecting the stars.

CHAPTER 14

Harvest Time: Sharing God's Bounty

If there's anything more joyful than a harvest, I don't know what it is. Every society in the world has celebrations and festivals centered on the miracle of harvest. It's impossible not to celebrate, because when you celebrate harvest, you celebrate life. But there is a danger. Some have built whole religions on harvest rituals, recognizing part of the miracle, but confusedly venerating the harvest instead of the One who caused the growth. Believe it or not, some Christians do the same. They celebrate the growth and good works in their lives instead of the One who caused the growth. If you wrapped up all the exciting harvest festivals you've ever seen into one glorious party, it wouldn't equal the passionate joy of a spiritual harvest. And it's perilously easy to forget where that growth came from and to praise it or yourself, instead of the Master Gardener, without whom you would still be a desert of choking dust. When you see fruit, look up! Praise His name with all the passion and gratitude you are capable of! He *did* it, when there were times you really wondered if He could. He brought forth the fruit of His holiness, in *you!* In *me!*

Here's a song to get you started. "Thou hast crowned the year with Thy bounty, and Thy paths drip with fatness. The pastures of the wilderness drip, and the hills gird themselves with rejoicing. The meadows are clothed with flocks, and the valleys are covered with grain; they shout for joy, yes, they sing" (Psalm 65:11-13). Now read all of the following psalm—Psalm 66. What praise!

Bearing fruit for God is the whole reason for our existence. Jesus said He had chosen us so that we might bear fruit, so that our prayers might be answered, and our joy might be full (see John 15:16; 16:24). In fact, Jesus taught a great deal about fruitfulness. First, He explained that our choices determine our fruit and that insistent and unrepentant choices to produce evil fruit would end in destruction. In Matthew 3:7-12 and Luke 3:8-17, John the Baptist laid the foundation, begging people to first produce fruit of repentance. In Matthew 7:16-20; 12:33; Luke 6:43-45, Jesus repeated the lesson. The fruit, good or bad, He insisted, is the result of a heart that has chosen for or against God as Master Gardener. He had good reason to keep repeating this lesson. He was surrounded by people who believed they were their own gardeners and that they could produce their own fruit apart from God. It could be said that they had created their own form of fertility religion. As long as they kept all the rules, they were fine and to be praised. If no one else praised them sufficiently, they praised themselves. Is this still true today?

In John 4, Jesus shows what true fruit really looks like. Speaking to the woman at the well, He promises the Holy Spirit, as the spring that will bubble up continuously in the consecrated soul " 'to eternal life' " (verse 14). Then He gives her the next step: to worship in Spirit and in truth— that is, to make worship a continuous lifestyle (see verses 23, 24). Verses 28-42 show the fruit beginning already. Who is fed by this encounter? The woman, of course. Then her fellow townspeople. But did you catch it? Look at verses 32-34. *Jesus* was so deeply "fed" and satisfied that even His physical hunger, which had not been touched, receded! He said that He had reaped and that His disciples could also reap, *"fruit for life eternal"* and that He and they would rejoice together! (See verses 36-38.)

John chapters 13–17 contain what I call the "last will and testament of Jesus Christ." Here He goes more deeply into the concept of fruit and harvest. As we noted above, He says that He has chosen these men to bear fruit. He has, of course, hundreds, maybe thousands, of other followers as well. And in His prayer in John 17, He speaks of all those who will believe through these (see John 17:20). In several places in these chapters, He hints at joys untold, at greater things the Spirit will teach them and do in them when He is gone back to His Father. Later, Paul and others recognize Jesus Himself as a kind of firstfruit (see 1 Corinthians 15:20-24). The apostles also speak of themselves and the early church as firstfruits. Paul says the gospel is bearing fruit and increasing in all the world (see Colossians 1:6). In the centuries since then, spreading like dandelions, Jesus' gardens have covered the whole earth. There's no stopping them!

In this same passage, Paul alludes to two levels of gardening. The fruit the gospel is bearing in the world clearly represents the people themselves—converts whom God is harvesting. In this picture, the Christian workers are planters and reapers. Then Paul adds that the gospel has been bearing fruit "in you also since the day you heard of it *and understood the grace of God in truth*" (verse 6, emphasis supplied). I italicized that phrase because it shows the essential protection against a works-based "fertility" religion. We must first understand grace and that the growth comes entirely from God. Paul continues: "We have not ceased to pray for you and to ask that you may be filled with the knowledge of His will in all spiritual wisdom and understanding, so that you may walk in a manner worthy of the Lord, to please Him in all respects, bearing fruit in every good work and increasing in the knowledge of God" (verses 9, 10). At this level, the fruit is growing inside an individual person and is defined as wisdom, understanding, good works, and knowledge of God.

Paul and his contemporaries, because of the incarnation of God in Christ, had a new understanding of this truth, but it was not a new thought. Proverbs contained the same two levels. "The root of the righteous yields fruit" (Proverbs 12:12). "The fruit of the righteous is a tree of life, and he who is wise wins souls" (Proverbs 11:30).

On the whole, our view of the garden of the soul in these pages has been introspective. We have hinted at growing friendships and at the sharing that comes naturally when the Gardener begins to work in our gardens. But we've been mostly concerned with the development of our own devotional lives. Harvest time is the time when we really understand why the garden of the soul is so important. We are not growing all this fruit for ourselves, or even for God's satisfaction. His satisfaction, which is much richer than we can imagine, comes from the joy of having more to feed all His other hungry children. Look again at John 4:32-42. When Jesus says, " 'I have food to eat that you do not know about,' " He continues immediately with a picture of the harvest. He knows He has just gained, not only a lonely woman, but a whole town! These Samaritans, unlike Jesus' own countrymen, beg Him to stay, and they actually listen! Have you ever really taken in the significance of verse 42? I'm not sure I have. "They were saying to the woman, 'It is no longer because of what you said that we believe, for we have heard for ourselves and know that *this One is indeed the Savior of the world'* " (emphasis supplied). They accepted Him completely as the Messiah! That's shocking! The disciples themselves took a long time in coming to that point and lost all hope when He died and all their dreams of an earthly kingdom were shattered.

What a harvest Jesus had that day! This is the goal of all our silent inner struggles. It's not just about us. It's not even about our own growth. It's about having something to share, something that will really fill and satisfy those starving souls we see on every side. As we carefully guard and nourish our hearts to keep them healthy, since out of them "flow the springs of life" (Proverbs 4:23), the fruit that they produce begins there. The thoughts of our hearts begin to twine more and more strongly around our Master. Then the fruit grows into our lives in two major ways, called by the Bible the fruit of our mouth and the fruit of our hands.

THE FRUIT OF THE MOUTH

Proverbs 13:2 says, "From the fruit of a man's mouth he enjoys good." The marginal reference says that the word translated "enjoys" is literally "eats." What is the fruit of the mouth? Words, of course. What comes out of the mouth is the first visible indication of what lives and grows in the heart. There are many more specifics here in Proverbs. For instance: "The one who guards his mouth preserves his life; the one who opens wide his lips comes to ruin" (verse 3). In other words, don't put your mouth in motion until you get your brain in gear. I once heard a preacher say, "You are only as good a Christian as you are when someone cuts in front of you in traffic." Ouch! Then there's verse 5: "A righteous man hates falsehood." Of course, there are lots of ways to lie, but the quickest and most common is in words. Here's Jesus' brother, James, on the subject. "The tongue is a small part of the body, and yet it boasts of great things. Behold, how great a forest is set aflame by such a small fire!" (James 3:5). Given the fact that Jesus' brothers did not originally believe in Him, is it possible that memories of their boyhood together might have come to mind as James wrote this? Had he, perhaps, been unkind with his words?

If you find crossness, unkindness, insults, or lies coming from your mouth, *don't* try to change the fruit of your mouth. Look to your heart! Go back to step one. Ask forgiveness, spend time in His presence, then begin looking for promises of good fruits like the ones above and hold them close, cultivate them, and to your amazement, the words will change. "With the fruit of a man's mouth his stomach will be satisfied; he will be satisfied with the product of his lips" (Proverbs 18:20). Don't think it's a small thing. God created the whole universe with His word; our words are tiny reflections of that power, for good or evil, subject to our free choice. "Death and life are in the power of the tongue, and those who love it will eat its fruit" (Proverbs 18:21).

This is what God promises: " 'I have seen his ways, but I will heal him; I will lead him and restore comfort to him and to his mourners, creating the praise of the lips. Peace, peace to him who is far and to him who is near,' says the Lord, 'and I will heal him' " (Isaiah 57:18, 19).

Praise of the lips! I know what it feels like to know that my lips have caused pain and suffering to people that I love, and yet to be forgiven and changed and to have people actually blessing me instead! I couldn't begin to describe the feeling, but I assure you it is very humbling. There is no hint of doubt that it all comes from God alone and from His work in my life.

THE FRUIT OF THE HANDS

Going back to Proverbs, we find the promise to the godly woman: "Give her the product of her hands, and let her works praise her in the gates" (Proverbs 31:31). Those who think the Bible teaches that women are second-class citizens who stay meekly at home should study this chapter closely. This woman is the chief of her large household in a way that bears little resemblance to our well-worn phrase "just a housewife." Besides everything else, she runs a business, deals with the merchants of her city and with salesmen. According to this verse, she should keep her own profits and be known in the gates, which were the courts, the Wall Street, and the public media of the day! Let me hasten to say that, like the rest of the promises of the Bible, this goes for men, too. When the heart is right, the fruit of the thoughts will be wholesome, which will lead to wholesome words and to productive actions—the fruit of the hands. And they will be recognized by all within one's circle of influence. Paradoxically, these fruits, produced so abundantly by a consecrated Christian, are often not recognized by himself. He is too busy paying attention to the heart, working silently with his Master Gardener, watching those skillful hands accomplish their miracles on stony soil and brittle branches. When someone praises the fruit of his hands, he smiles and points them to his Gardener, recommending that they, too, sell Him their garden and watch what will happen.

Not only will the fruits of our lives be noticed and recognized by other people, but they will be rewarded by God as well. "Say to the righteous that it will go well with them, for they will eat the fruit of their actions. Woe to the wicked! It will go badly with him, for what he deserves will be done to him" (Isaiah 3:10). " 'I, the Lord, search the heart, I test the mind, even to give to each man according to his ways' " (Jeremiah 17:10). People have been scared and messed up by passages like this since Satan convinced Eve there was more knowledge to be had outside of God than in Him. If you don't know the Gardener, what are you to do? Desperately tie figs to your dead branches, so an angry God will be fooled into thinking you are alive, and not curse you? It has never worked, and it never will. Let Him in, and let Him do His own gardening. Then your works will be His works which "God prepared beforehand, that [you] should walk in them" (Ephesians 2:10). The rewards you'll get, whether here or in heaven, will be rightfully His, too, which makes the whole thing rather unfair. He does all the work, and you get all the benefits—but He doesn't mind. His reward is your heart-swelling praise. Others might think you're really something, but you know the truth, and you make sure God and others know you know.

Revelation 20 makes some very important points about the concept of being judged by our works or by the fruit of our hands. You'll find that the righteous are always said to be "rewarded" according to their works (sometimes earthly rewards are being spoken of and sometimes heavenly ones), but in Revelation 20 the dead are said to be "judged" according to their deeds (verse 12). What's the difference? Well, we need to have a clear understanding of the context. In verses 4-6, John shows the resurrection of the worshipers of God—"those who had not worshipped the beast or his image" (verse 4)—in other words, Satan, or any of his false systems created in his own evil image. "Blessed," says John, "and holy is the one who has a part in the first resurrection; over these the second death has no power." In fact, they "reign with [Christ]" (verse 6).

So, in verse 12, when the judgment is set up, the books are opened, and "the dead, the great and the small" stand before the great white throne to hear their sentences, who are these dead? The righteous dead have already been raised to life, so these can only be the wicked dead. They, the Bible says, will be "judged from the things which were written in the books, according to their deeds" (verse 12). Now, why? Think about it. There are, and have always been, only two choices: accept Jesus' payment of the penalty for your sins or insist that, no thank you, you can stand on your own two feet and pay for your own sins. These people made the latter choice, and will now pay for their own sins just as they wanted to. The result, terrible to contemplate, is shown clearly in verses 14 and 15. "Death and Hades were thrown into the lake of fire. This is the second [or eternal] death, the lake of fire. And if anyone's name was not found written in the book of life, he was thrown into the lake of fire."

That day is not yet, praise God. He is still waiting, wishing that none at all would choose to be lost. And in Hosea 14, He pleadingly, insistently states His case. This is so beautiful that I want to reproduce the whole chapter here. (The italics in verse 8 are mine.) Put your own name in the place of Israel or Ephraim, and any sin or self-dependence that has caused you to stumble, in the place of Assyria or horses or idols.

> Return, O Israel, to the Lord your God,
> For you have stumbled because of your iniquity.
> Take words with you and return to the Lord.
> Say to Him, "Take away all iniquity,
> And receive us graciously,
> That we may present the fruit of our lips.
> Assyria will not save us,
> We will not ride on horses;
> Nor will we say again, 'Our god,'
> To the work of our hands;
> For in Thee the orphan finds mercy."

> I will heal their apostasy,
> I will love them freely,
> For My anger has turned away from them.
> I will be like the dew to Israel;
> He will blossom like the lily,
> And he will take root like the cedars of Lebanon.
> His shoots will sprout,
> And his beauty will be like the olive tree,
> And his fragrance like the cedars of Lebanon.
> Those who live in his shadow
> Will again raise grain,
> And they will blossom like the vine.
> His renown will be like the wine of Lebanon.

> O Ephraim, what more have I to do with idols?
> *It is I who answer and look after you.*
> *I am like a luxuriant cypress;*
> *From Me comes your fruit.*

Whoever is wise, let him understand these things;
Whoever is discerning, let him know them.
For the ways of the Lord are right,
And the righteous will walk in them,
But transgressors will stumble in them.

Take His words to heart. Let Him live and move and have His being within you, and you will grow into the complete and perfect fullness of the fruit of the Spirit. Then God will throw a harvest party, and you will join in the celebration as you never have before, because you'll see sheaves gathered into His kingdom that you feared would never be there. He can do it!

DIG DEEPER

List some of the errors fertility religions have fallen into. Then compare them with the errors Christians can fall into by watching for, measuring, looking up to, and celebrating works or good deeds in the life instead of God, who causes good deeds.

Praise God for some of the fruit and growth He's caused in your life. If you like, use Psalms 65 and 66 as templates to write Him a song of praise and thanksgiving. How has His fruit blessed you? How has it blessed others? Have you had the blessed joy of seeing human souls harvested partly because of the fruit God has grown in your life? If so, praise Him for the awesome privilege! If not, wait until the final harvest. You might be surprised!

How is the fruit of your mouth? Is it showing the presence of Jesus in your life? If not, what can you do about it?

What are some words that have brought life to your heart this week? Remember to thank the person who spoke them.

Are there words for which you need to ask forgiveness?

In what ways have you received the fruit of your hands? Do you dedicate all that your hands may do to God every day?

What do you do when your labor appears to be completely unfruitful?

Snapshots From My Garden

At first, the chill was a welcome relief from the long, sweaty days of labor. She breathed in the crisp air and relished the freshness. Then she began to see new colors in her garden—red and gold where there had been green. It was breathtaking, and she invited her friends to share it.

One day the Gardener told her that if she had thought they were busy before, she had seen nothing yet. They had to begin "putting by."

"Putting by?"

"Yes. Storing the fruits of our labors for long, cold, barren times."

"Barren? But I thought the garden would produce all of our needs now!"

"No, the winter is coming, and the garden must rest."

She was bewildered, but trusting. She had learned He always knew what He was doing. She went to work, helping Him can, freeze, dry, store. . . . It was endless! Even the cool days grew sweaty and breathless. They built shelves and dug root cellars and filled them to the brim.

Then came the freeze. She had never known before that something could be incredibly beautiful and somehow terrifying at the same time. It was cold! Her flowers froze and withered; the vine over the trellis grew brown and brittle; the vegetables and grains were no more. And her tree—her tree lost its greenness and even some of its leaves!

She was frightened, and when she tried to ask the Gardener what was happening, as they sat in their swing together, he seemed preoccupied and distant. "Wait," was all He would say. "Be patient."

Be patient! So she waited. And she was patient.

Day after day, the chill grew. She shivered in unaccustomed winds and ate dried and canned food. The garden looked almost as barren as it had in those other days—before. Even the spring froze around the edges.

Her Tree looked dead.

"Master?"

He said nothing.

She continued to wait. But her patience grew frazzled. An ice storm broke some branches off her Tree, and they hung there, unattended, dry and gray.

She found herself crying and skipping meetings at the swing. Her friends didn't come to the gate. Why should they? It was cold and ugly there!

"Master!" she cried, sometimes even screamed. "Why won't You talk to me?"

Sobbing under the trellis one day, she heard a voice. She looked up. It was her truest friend, Grace. Grace put her arms around her and listened to her disjointed tale of woe and desolation. Then she asked, "What has the Master Gardener said?"

"That's just it!" she wailed. "He's deserted me!"

"Deserted you!" Grace looked shocked. "Doesn't He come to the swing to meet with you?"

She looked away. "I don't know. I haven't been there lately."

"Then how can you say it's He who has deserted you?"

"When I did go, He wouldn't even talk to me! All He said was wait! Be patient! I did, and look where that got me!"

"Oh, so He did say something?"

"Well, sure, if you call that talking. He had told me before that there would be winter and that the garden had to rest. But this doesn't look like a rest! This looks like death! Doesn't He love me anymore?" She sank into bitter sobbing once more.

Grace held her and waited. When the storm had quieted a little, she asked, "Do you have enough to eat?"

"Yes, the stores are getting low, but there is still plenty."

"Why?" asked Grace.

"Because He—we—put by a lot of stuff."

"And you really believe He could stop loving you?"

She thought back. She remembered His hard work. His endless patience with her mistakes. His insistence that they fill all those shelves and pits. His scarred hands. His warm, strong arms. His eyes. "No," she whispered.

"Then He must have some purpose, don't you think? I've noticed He doesn't always explain everything. Don't you think you might just trust Him, as you've learned to do?"

She sat up and blew her nose. "I guess so. Yes. I will. If you'll excuse me, I'm going to our meeting place at the swing." She started to walk, then turned. "Grace? Thank you!"

Grace smiled. It was strange—her smile was almost like the Gardener's.

At the swing, she saw Him, sitting alone. She sat down beside Him. He didn't look at her, so she said, "Can't You talk to me yet? Well, I just want You to know, I trust You anyway. I do. I'll wait and try to be patient."

There was silence, then His arm, warm and strong as ever, came around her. She leaned back into it, and they sat together, not speaking. After a while, she realized they didn't really need to speak. Just to be together.

She looked up. There were tiny yellow buds on the tree.

CHAPTER 15

Seasons and Cycles: The Circle of Life

Since we have only from sun to sun, a gardener's work is never done (to twist an old saw)! You just finish sneezing from the dust kicked up by the heavy equipment, when there's building to do. You get a little ahead with that, and there's digging. Then planting, and then weeding, mulching, watering, followed by more—much more—of all of the above. Often all at the same time. One bed is just beginning to sprout, another is overgrown, another needs division, and the Master Gardener has just decided that a pond would look great right *there*. Or that you need a new potting shed or another bench.

As the season progresses, the work gets heavier and more overwhelming. You have canning and drying and sharing.... And then, suddenly—or so it seems—frost arrives, and everything comes to a grinding halt. It's winter.

In the physical world we understand that winter is a necessity of life if we live in a temperate zone. As just one of many examples, if you don't get a freeze, you won't get apples. We even welcome the break. For a while. Then we start getting cold, then bored, then restless. Will spring *ever* come? To comfort ourselves, we get lost in bright, summery seed catalogs from January on.

But what about the spiritual world? Is there really a winter there? Is it a good thing? We flawed humans are so inexperienced in the spiritual world—our vision is so blurry there, we're such babies there—that we panic easily. Aren't we supposed to bear fruit all the time? Isn't that the sign of a healthy spiritual life? If we have a dry spell, a barren spell, worse yet, a cold spell, doesn't that meant we've lost contact with the Vine?

I will confess in advance that I expect this to be the most difficult chapter of this whole book for me to write. I've struggled with these questions for years on end. If my heart felt dry, if it seemed no growth was going on, then I felt that it must be because of a lack in my devotional life. So I would try to infuse my daily devotions with new life, new determination. And when that didn't "work" (that is, I didn't see the growth and virtue that I expected), I used to find myself fading away from it entirely. Pretty soon I wasn't having devotions at all. Then, I could easily make a simple diagnosis. It was all my fault! I was right! I must have had a defective devotional life, which meant I didn't *really* love God as I should. You can see where this sort of thinking would lead.

This has happened over and over in my personal life. But the Gardener never let go of me, and I (an important point!) never let go of Him. He led me to the writings of godly people who said they struggled with the same thing. They said there were seasons in the Christian life, and that winter, or a dry spell, in and of itself, didn't mean we were disconnected from God. I turned and looked back, and I saw it was true! So little by little, I'm learning some things I am about to share with you. But I warn you, I'm still only on the kindergarten level. You could probably tell me more than I can tell you. Perhaps you will, and the dialogue Gordon MacDonald wished for in his book *Ordering Your Inner World* will continue. I hope so!

Where do we look when we have questions about the world of the spirit? To our friends, our pastors, to Gordon MacDonald, Morris Venden, Ellen White, George Mueller? Maybe. Sometimes. But first, last, and always, we need to go to the real Gardeners' Manual—the

Bible. I suspected those writers I read were right, but I had to have it confirmed by the Word of God.

Let's start in Psalm 1. This psalm says the righteous will be "like a tree firmly planted by streams of water, which yields its fruit *in its season*" (verse 3, emphasis supplied). I hadn't noticed that before until I went looking for it! And I didn't go looking for it until I began to research this book. I thought I was going to write a book about how the Christian life could be *always* fruitful. Isn't it amazing how God leads? Let's look at this psalm. It goes on to say that this tree's "leaf does not wither" (verse 3). Interesting. That means the tree of my life is an evergreen. I never thought of it that way. In fact, I considered going back and changing this book to make it one, but I decided that sharing my growth with you as it happens might be more valuable to both of us. So we have an evergreen tree. Why, then, have I seen some leaves (or needles) fall? Right outside my window as I write, are several huge evergreens—a cedar, a spruce, a red pine, and farther away, acres of white pines. They do lose some needles every year. But they don't wither, and they always stay green unless they're diseased or dying. That must be the way Jesus plans for our spiritual gardens to be. Maybe there are times of rest and recharging—times when we might lose some old needles. But we won't really wither or die, as long as we are planted by living waters.

Let's go back to our psalm and see what makes a person's life like this evergreen tree with living water at its roots. Beginning at verse 1 again, we see that this person does not walk in the counsel of the wicked, stand in the path of sinners, or sit in the seat of scoffers. Have I ever walked, sat, or stood that way? Yes, I certainly have! And the result was always disease and the beginning of death. What's the remedy? "But his delight is in the law of the Lord, and in His law he meditates day and night" (verse 2). Ah! A breakthrough!

I've been in two different kinds of dry spell.

1. A dry spell that came about because I was neglecting my devotional life. This is simple to remedy, though not necessarily easy. I seek out the Gardener; I tell Him how sorry I am and how much I miss

Him; and I go back to spending time alone with Him. The dryness fades into green growth, and the joy comes back.

2. A dry spell that came about for no reason that I could see, despite a faithful devotional life. My response has usually been to try to "do something" more perfectly than before, and if I don't see immediate growth, to get discouraged, which leads to missed devotional times. What happens? More brittle dryness, more disease, more death! This psalm says that the person who meditates on God and His character, or law, day and night, is the one who will not wither! What? Not even in dry spells? No, but he will yield fruit only *in its season.*

If it were a physical reality, we wouldn't even think twice. We would know there were different types of growth for different times. Why don't we recognize that in the spiritual realm? As Ecclesiastes 3 points out, there is a time for everything—times for planting and for uprooting are specifically mentioned. I've learned there are times for me to be producing and times to be quietly recharging myself. If I neglect the one, the other becomes impossible. Notice the last phrase in Psalm 1:3: "Whatever he does, he prospers." I used to scoff at that. It sounds as if it means that everything he tries will succeed. I know that's not true! But what if it means that whether he's growing, budding, putting out new needles, making tiny cones, dropping full-grown cones to feed those who depend on him, or silently waiting out the winter and dropping old needles, his times are in the hands of His Gardener, and he can stand, firmly planted, drinking the water of life, and knowing that he is fulfilling a purpose greater than he can see?

How awesome! And that's only one passage!

How about the principle of "putting by," saving food for barren seasons? Is it biblical?

"Thy word I have treasured in my heart, that I may not sin against Thee" (Psalm 119:11).

" 'Lay up for yourselves treasures in heaven, where neither moth nor rust destroys, and where thieves do not break in or steal; for where your treasure is, there will your heart be also' " (Matthew 6:20, 21).

"His mother [Mary] treasured all these things in her heart" (Luke 2:51).

" 'The good man out of the good treasure of his heart brings forth what is good; and the evil man out of the evil treasure brings forth what is evil' " (Luke 6:45). Note that this verse comes right after a treatise on good and bad trees and fruit.

And look at this! " 'Have you understood all these things?' They said to Him, 'Yes.' And He said to them, 'Therefore every scribe who has become a disciple of the kingdom of heaven is like a head of a household, who brings forth out of his treasure things new and old' " (Matthew 13:51, 52). I never understood this verse until just this minute! I am a scribe by trade, and as a disciple of the Master, I have been treasuring the things He has given me for years. Now I am sharing with you, "things new and old"! I can't think of anything in life more exciting! But what if I hadn't put treasures by when I had them to spare?

Sometimes a dry spell becomes more than just a season. Sometimes it goes on and on until it's a full-blown drought. It comes to the point that you feel you've used up all you put by, and there's nothing left. I've felt that way before. Have you? That brings us to our next passage—the ultimate story of what a faithful caretaker is supposed to do when his garden seems completely bare and dead. It's the story of Habakkuk.

All of this small book is worthwhile reading. The third chapter is especially poignant. Not only is every horrifying thing that could possibly happen crashing over Habakkuk's life, but it is happening at the hand of God. His nation has turned decidedly from Him, and God is on the warpath. But not every child in the nation has turned from God. Some just got in the way of the consequences. Have you ever felt like that? I have. I have also been on the receiving end of judgments I knew I thoroughly deserved. Habakkuk has poured out his heart and his feelings, his terror, in this book. Here is the finale: "I heard and my inward parts trembled, at the sound my lips quivered. Decay enters my bones, and in my place I tremble. Because I must wait quietly for the day of distress, for the people to arise who will invade us" (Habakkuk 3:16). I recognize that horrible sense of dread—waiting helplessly for what you know you cannot stop. Habakkuk then ends with this incredible prayer: "Though the fig tree should not blossom, and there be no fruit on the vines, though the yield of the olive should fail, and the fields produce no food, though the flock should be cut off from the fold, and there be no cattle in the stalls, yet I will exult in the Lord, I will rejoice in the God of my salvation. The Lord God is my strength, and He has made my feet like hinds' feet, and makes me walk on my high places" (verses 17-19).

This may be the most powerful prayer a child of God could pray. Habakkuk is saying, *"Even though it seems God's own covenant promises are failing, even though there is nothing put by, nothing to eat, even if I die, I will praise You, and I will rejoice."*

I wonder if perhaps we all have to come to that moment. I know I had to come, through great personal trial, to a night when I stood outside in the dark and looked up at an empty sky and said, with tears pouring down my face, "There is no evidence that You are even here or care. I cannot see, hear, or sense You in any way. My prayers are answered with silence. I don't know how You can expect me to have faith in You. I wouldn't trust a human who treated me as You do for one second. But I am too stubborn to give You up! I could not live without You! If You don't exist, then I'll die a fool, but I won't give You up. I still believe, and I'll still praise You. I *know* You have a plan! I know it."

I've heard a lot of other stories like mine too. Here's one.

"The silences of Jesus are as eloquent as His speech and may be a sign, not of His disapproval, but of His approval and of a deep purpose of blessing for you.... Listen to an old and beautiful story of how one Christian dreamed that she saw three others at prayer. As they knelt the Master drew near to them.

"As He approached the first of the three, He bent over her in tenderness and grace, with smiles full of radiant love and spoke to her in accents of purest, sweetest music.

"Leaving her, He came to the next, but only placed His hand upon her bowed head and gave her one look of loving approval.

"The third woman He passed almost abruptly without stopping for a word or glance. The woman in her dream said to herself, 'How greatly He must love the first one. To the second He gave His approval, but none of the special demonstrations of love He gave the first. And the third must have grieved Him deeply, for He gave her no word at all and not even a passing look.

" 'I wonder what she has done, and why He made so much difference between them?' As she tried to account for the action of her Lord, He Himself stood by her and said: 'O woman! how wrongly hast thou interpreted Me. The first kneeling woman needs all the weight of My tenderness and care to keep her feet in My narrow way. She needs My love, thought, and help every moment of the day. Without it she would fail and fall.

" 'The second has stronger faith and deeper love, and I can trust her to trust Me however things may go and whatever people do.

" 'The third, whom I seemed not to notice and even to neglect, has faith and love of the finest quality, and her I am training by quick and drastic measures for the highest and holiest service.

" 'She knows Me so intimately, and trusts Me so utterly, that she is independent of words or looks or any outward intimation of My approval. She is not dismayed nor discouraged by any circumstances through which I arrange that she shall pass; she trusts Me when sense and reason and every finer instinct of the natural heart would rebel because she knows that I am working in her for eternity, and that what I do, though she knows not the explanation now, she will understand hereafter.

" 'I am silent in My love because I love beyond the power of words to express or of human hearts to understand, and also for your sakes that you may learn to love and trust Me in Spirit-taught, spontaneous response to My love, without the spur of anything outward to call it forth.'

"He will do marvels if you will learn the mystery of His silence, and praise Him, for every time He withdraws His gifts that you may better know and love the Giver" (Mrs. Charles E. Cowman, *Streams in the Desert*, pp. 53, 54).

This story helped me very much when I was in my own barren desert. However, there is one clarification I would like to make. Like every other human to whom God speaks, this writer was trying to describe a supernatural lesson in human language, and I believe he or she made one statement that could be misunderstood. *Every* Christian needs Jesus' love and help every moment to keep from falling—not just the weak ones. It is clear that this writer meant that weak ones need more outward demonstration from Jesus of that love and help. All three women were being helped and held every second, but only one *felt* it. Ah! Feelings! How wonderful it is when we clearly feel Him near! When we don't feel Him, we are so tempted to think He isn't there. He is trying to train us to know that He is always by our side, whether we feel Him or not.

Winters and dry spells are the times when we can learn that. They always end, sooner or later. " 'I will seek the lost, bring back the scattered, bind up the broken, and strengthen the sick,' " says our Master (Ezekiel 34:16). In this passage He is speaking as a shepherd, but the image holds for our garden, too. The ice has shown which branches were weak by breaking them off. The dryness has caused the older needles and leaves to fall. The wind has scattered the chaff, and if there is anything useful, that has been lost or blown away, He'll find it. If any illness has shown up, He'll heal it. Spring will come again and the fullness of summer and the surplus of autumn. Then the round will begin all over again.

> The righteous [one] will flourish like the palm tree,
> He will grow a cedar in Lebanon.
> Planted in the house of the Lord,
> They will flourish in the courts of our God.
> They will still yield fruit in old age;
> They shall be full of sap and very green,
> To declare that the Lord is upright;
> He is my rock, and there is no unrighteousness in Him
> (Psalm 92:12-15).

DIG DEEPER

Looking back, can you see winters and droughts in your spiritual life? When were they your own fault, and when were they not? What made the difference? What was your reaction in each case, and what were the results?

What season are you living through now? What is God accomplishing in it? Are you trusting Him totally? How can you trust Him even more than you do now?

Study Psalm 1 or another passage on fruit in season, and ask God how He wants you to put the teachings you find into practice in your life today and tomorrow.

What treasures have you "put by" to hold you through winters and dry spells? Are you sure you have enough to last you? Determine a program of memorization that is practical for you and put it into practice. You might practice with a friend.

Study the book of Habakkuk, especially if you are undergoing a time of trouble like his. Compare the losses he lists with the covenant promises in Deuteronomy and elsewhere. How do you think Habakkuk felt when He saw what appeared to be the failure of God Himself to fulfill His own promises? Have you ever felt like that? If so, pray Habakkuk's prayer with him, and like him, stay on the walls watching for the blessing you can be *sure* will come.

Which of the women in the dream are you most like, and why?

Snapshots From My Garden

They sat together on the swing, their shoulders touching, swinging gently in the late afternoon sunshine. She held a sprig of herb in her hand, brushing her fingers over its narrow leaves to make it give off its rich fragrance. "Rosemary for remembrance," she mused.

*"Remember," said the Gardener solemnly, " 'the ways by which you went.' " ***

Her mind drifted back, all the way back to "before." Her memory was fuzzy now, out of focus like an old picture. Mostly, she remembered darkness and cold. She shivered and pressed closer to His warm shoulder. How had she survived, she and her spindly plants, her poor, weak tree that she had thought of in capital letters in those days—the Tree of Her Life, the be-all and end-all of her lonely existence? She had tried so hard to care for it, yet she had refused it sunshine, air, even water. She looked up at it now, swaying above them strong and healthy, and smiled.

"I remember when You first came and knocked. I nearly died of fright. And then You called me by my own name and ripped out a board so we could see each other!" She laughed. "If I had known then what You had planned, I would have died! Tearing everything down, hauling away all my precious treasures . . . I thought You were crazy, You know."

He was smiling too. "I am. By the standards of this world, I am most assuredly insane."

"And so am I, now!" she agreed, leaning her head on His shoulder. She looked along the length of the jeweled lapis wall, so much longer than the old wall on which she had worked so hard. It encompassed infinitely more area. The ruby-encrusted watchtower—where she had taken refuge during the cold of the winter and during the storms that sometimes came—sparkled in the sunshine. The crystal gate was a dear, familiar meeting place now, surrounded by flowers, with cushioned benches under the arbor, and well-worn stepping stones. It seemed strange now, how frightened she used to be of people.

"Let's walk," suggested the Gardener, and they rose and slowly paced through their garden.

They made wreaths for each other's heads from the flowerbeds, looked eagerly for swelling baby fruit on the espaliered trees, and admired the grain field, growing green and tall again. They walked barefoot on the lush grass, made plans for the briar patch, and wandered through the vegetable garden, planning supper by what they found there. They pinched a few herbs just to spice up the breeze, and ended up by the spring, where they took a drink and lay on their backs in the cool grotto of ferns and lady-slippers.

"Who would ever have imagined?" she sighed in the deepest contentment.

The Master Gardener smiled and touched her cheek. "I would," He said. He sent a gaze that seemed full of secrets up to the sky. "Just you wait and see," He added. "We've only just begun."

*Jeremiah 31:21.

CHAPTER 16

God's Estates: The Ultimate Landscape Plan

We've barely scratched the surface of God's gardening. We've spent a whole book on one small aspect—God's "mini gardens" in individual hearts. Each of us can be one of those little gardens, and every one of us will be different. Some of us are lamp-post gardens, standing tall and shining God's light into the darkness. Some are mailbox gardens, sending the good news through long distance means from our solitary spot. Some are shade gardens, offering shelter and comfort to hot, weary travelers on the road of life. Some are window boxes, maybe blooming for just one person or just one family. The possibilities are limited only by the Master Gardener's imagination.

But we all have some things in common. We take the time on an ongoing basis to live and move and have our being within the Gardener's hands and under His hoe and pruning shears. We are learning to let Him plant, cultivate, and harvest whatever, whenever, and wherever He desires. We wield any gardening tool He asks us to and listen for His voice to tell us how long, how deep, and when to stop.

And when our inner gardens, once a place of panic and despair, have grown and developed enough order that we are able to look up and around, we discover that we are only one tiny part of God's immense and lovely estate, and that He has plans we haven't begun to dream. God's master landscape plan includes the whole world and the whole universe. There are at least four levels of planting in which He is involved. First He plants in individuals. The greatest gardens are all made up of single plants, and when the single plants are not healthy, the garden is not healthy. Then He plants those individuals in groups, and plants the groups in security and love. Then He teaches us to help plant in others, so that the growth and joy will spread. Ultimately, God's gardens will cover the earth. And finally, the Bible says, He will plant the heavens. In this final chapter, we will take a look at each of these levels of planting, and I pray that each of us will find a glimpse of some of the plans God may have for us.

GOD PLANTS IN INDIVIDUALS

This has been the subject of this book. It will be enough now to wrap it up with the quintessential parable on the matter—the parable of the sower. This story is found in Matthew 13:1-23 and Luke 8:4-15. In this parable, Jesus defines the sower as Himself, the seed as the Word of God, and the soil as individual hearts. He goes into detail with His disciples about three categories of trouble that can stunt a garden's growth, or stop it altogether.

1. Roadside—sheer lack of understanding, or indifference. This person hears the Word, but it flies right over his head. Or he doesn't think it applies to him or that it's important. The devil, says Jesus, steals the seed before it can even sprout. The Gardener can do nothing in this garden until He is let in, and He will not be let in until the person hears, understands, and accepts for himself the Word of God. This is not likely to happen except in one way—through the fervent, imploring prayers of those around him, and the sharing of fruit from their gardens until he begins to see this fruit might be a good thing to have after all.

2. Rocky soil—this person hears, understands, gets all excited, then goes on her merry way. She doesn't understand she must let the Gar-

dener in and live with Him *daily,* learning to let Him work, and to work with Him. When trouble comes—and it does, without delay—she gives up easily. There's an interesting and hopeful aspect to this particular problem. Lots of us happy, healthy gardens used to be this way. We looked hopeless. But when a plant dies among the stones, it leaves a little organic matter. The next time the same thing happens, it leaves a little more. Eventually, there is enough soil in the rocks to hold a little water, and grow a little root, and growth finally begins. That's why Jesus doesn't give up. This, too, is helped mightily by prayer and sharing from nearby healthy gardens.

3. Thorns—this person hears, understands, accepts, and begins to grow. Trouble, of course, comes along—or success, depending on which the enemy thinks will be more likely to choke this soul whom he's been studying since birth. Thorny cares and worries, or shiny, sleek riches and pleasures—it doesn't matter which, so long as it is fast-growing, and entangling. Now comes the crucial moment. The Gardener wants to do some weed-whacking, some digging, even some burning. Will the person accept this, even learn to help with it, or will he turn away in fear or unwillingness? The decision may hinge on whether or not he has seen someone else nearby who has undergone the process and can speak glowingly of the results. And (you knew I was going to say this) prayer.

Jesus concludes with a description of the good soil. I particularly like the way it is put in Luke 8:15: " 'And the seed in the good soil, these are the ones who have heard the word in an honest and good heart, and hold it fast, and bear fruit with perseverance [marginal note: steadfastness].' " Did the thorns come? Yes. Did the birds come? Yes. Were there rocks? Yes. But this person *held fast* and didn't let go. Ask any gardener: Does good soil just happen? Neither does an honest heart. It grows over time as we live and work with our Master and never let go.

GOD PLANTS HIS PEOPLE IN SECURITY

In Amos 9:14, God makes a promise to a people who have been overwhelmed with thorns and destruction. He says, " 'I will restore the captivity of My people Israel, and they will rebuild the ruined cities and live in them, they will also plant vineyards and drink their wine, and make gardens and eat their fruit.' " That's what we've been learning about all the way through this book. Then God adds, " 'I will also plant them on their land, and they will not again be rooted out from their land which I have given them,' says the Lord your God" (verse 15).

There are many promises like this in the Bible, and we will look at several of them. What, exactly, do they mean? Were they just speaking temporally, of God's plans for His people Israel? Plans that never came to fruition, by the way, because the Israelites as a whole simply could not bring themselves to let God disentangle them from the thorns of circumstance and temptation and *stay* in His hands. Or do these promises have a spiritual application for spiritual Israel—you and me?

Let's look at some of these promises in Jeremiah. " ' "I will set My eyes on them for good, and I will bring them again to this land; and I will build them up and not overthrow them, and I will plant them and not pluck them up" ' " (Jeremiah 24:6). " 'Behold, days are coming,' declares the Lord, 'when I will sow the house of Israel and the house of Judah with the seed of man and with the seed of beast. And it will come about that as I have watched over them to pluck up, to break down, to overthrow, to destroy, and to bring disaster, so I will watch over them to build and to plant,' declares the Lord" (Jeremiah 31:27, 28). " 'And I will rejoice over them to do them good, and I will faithfully plant them in this land with all My heart and with all My soul' " (Jeremiah 32:41). God is speaking to Israel, and He is promising to give them their country back if they surrender to Him, right? Right! But could there be more? Could there be something for me?

I once claimed promises like these for land of my own. And they were fulfilled miraculously! I started a new life with three little children on five acres that were our own. I was transported by joy, for exactly three weeks. Then everything fell apart. We lost everything and were forcibly moved to a government apartment in a city neighborhood where fights, sullenness, and police presence were a daily reality. Now I had a hard choice to make. Would I still believe that God's plans for me were "good, and not evil"? Was he going to plant me somewhere safe and secure? Surely, I thought, this could not be the place! For some time, I refused to make the apartment my home. We lived there, and our furniture, such as it was, was there. But I hung no pictures, put no personal touches on the place. I grew sadder and sadder.

Finally I asked myself, "What is it you miss most about life in the country?" I decided it was gardens and animals. Could I bring those elements into this place where it appeared I had been planted, at least for now? I bought inexpensive department-store houseplants. A friend gave us a cage of finches. Another gave us an aquarium, and we began to collect fish we could afford, such as guppies and mollies.

One day at the store, we saw a six-foot weeping fig tree. I had always wanted a tree like that, but they cost a fortune. My son said, "Look, Mom! It's on sale!" It was only $25! Did I dare spend that much on a tree for my living room? My other son crawled around the base of the plant, and on the side of the pot he found a sticker. $12.50! I couldn't believe it!

"Let's take it!" I said daringly. So we wrestled it, as gently as possible, into the back of our little hatchback and brought it home.

A few days later, I sat in my special chair where I read my Bible. The branches of the fig hung over the back of my chair and filtered the sun shining through the window. The finches sang from the kitchen, and the water pumping through the aquarium gurgled and bubbled. I closed my eyes and imagined I was outside near a creek.

Instead of moving me, as I longed for Him to do, God moved *in* me. I knew He had worked His special magic once again, and the healing had begun.

If you go back to the verses in Jeremiah quoted above, you will find that right beside each of those promises, is another, different, promise. God says He will put His covenant in their hearts and live there inside of them. He is not just talking of planting Israelites in Israel (or of planting us where we'd like to be planted), and He is not just talking of our eventual reward in heaven. He is speaking of the temple, the garden sanctuary, He wants to build inside you and me, and live in. And He's saying He will plant us in security and peace forever. Does He mean no more thorns, no more battles, no more disease or pestilence or weeds? Yes, eventually, He means exactly that. But not yet. For now, He means He will fight the battles, tear out the thorns, soothe the pains, and control the weeds. " 'I will make a covenant of peace with them and eliminate harmful beasts from the land, so that they may live securely in the wilderness and sleep in the woods' " (Ezekiel 34:25). So you see, we are still in the wilderness, not yet out of the woods, but we can have peace. " 'I will make them and the places around My hill a blessing. And I will cause showers to come down in their season; they will be showers of blessing. Also the tree of the field will yield its fruit, and the earth will yield its increase, and they will be secure on their land. Then they will know that I am the Lord' " (verses 26, 27).

Like Moses, I didn't know God's No was preparing me for a bigger Yes than I had asked for or imagined. Today I live on thirty-seven acres, with a husband who loves me and with the last child at home. We have woods, fields, animals—even horses (a deep desire since childhood). We raise our own vegetables, milk, and eggs, and this year I'm starting an orchard and fruit garden. He has brought my feet out on a wide place, indeed. I understand now, better than I did then, that I had to learn to bloom where I was planted before I could be planted in a new place. If I had learned to be happy only after coming here, how would I know if it was true happiness or if it would end if I ever had to move away and lose this place? How would I know if it was happiness from the joy of having the Spirit in my heart or just pleasure of having things the way I want them?

The best thing about this new life is not the things and circumstances around me, but the work I have been given to do for the Master Gardener. And I don't believe I could do that work if I hadn't been through all the dark paths I've traveled.

That brings us to our next level of planting. When we have let God begin His gardening in our hearts, and when we have let Him plant us in security and peace under His watchful eye, despite what troubles we still experience in this wilderness, He will " 'make [us] … a blessing' " (Ezekiel 34:26).

GOD PLANTS IN OTHERS THROUGH US

In the parable of the sower, although Jesus says He is the Sower, it is also understood that His followers are sowers also, in the sense that they broadcast the seed He has entrusted to them. Paul asks, "How then shall they call upon Him in whom they have not believed? And how shall they believe in Him whom they have not heard? And how shall they hear without a preacher?… So faith comes from hearing, and hearing by the word of Christ" (Romans 10:14-17). We are called to sow the Word given to us. We are also called to humbly remember whose seed it is and who is causing any and all growth. "Neither the one who plants nor the one who waters is anything, but God who causes the growth. Now he who plants and he who waters are one; but each will receive his own reward according to his own labor. For we are God's fellow workers; you are God's field" (1 Corinthians 3:7-9).

No allegory is a perfect picture of the kingdom of God. It may be an interesting mix of metaphors that we are both the field in which God plants and also the sower in other fields, but that's one of those paradoxes God seems to enjoy. You can't even be a sower unless you're a well-plowed, fruitful field first. God could give you whole bags of seed, and sometimes He does. But usually, it seems He would rather plant in you, and let you grow your own seed to share. It's more meaningful that way as long as you never lose sight of His ownership and think you grew that seed all by yourself.

God's plan is that the individual mini gardens will spread and merge together into one huge garden that will cover the world.

GOD PLANTS THE WHOLE EARTH

" 'The surviving remnant of the house of Judah shall again take root downward and bear fruit upward' " (Isaiah 37:31). "In the days to come Jacob will take root, Israel will blossom and sprout; and they will fill the whole world with fruit" (Isaiah 27:6). As is always true of the Bible, these passages have layers of meaning. God was making promises to individual believers and to the nation of Israel as a whole, but He was also making a very specific and special promise to the whole earth. Isaiah

11:1, 2 says, "A shoot will spring forth from the stem of Jesse, and a branch from his roots will bear fruit. And the Spirit of the Lord will rest on Him, the spirit of wisdom and understanding, the spirit of counsel and strength, the spirit of knowledge and the fear of the Lord." As you continue reading this beautiful passage, you will find it describes the Son of God in passionate detail. So in an indescribable, powerful way, God planted Himself in His people by sending His own Son as a branch from *our* roots! Impossible! Until God did it. Then Jesus became the Vine, as He explains in John 15, and we can become *His* branches and bear *His* fruit. Then He gives us His living Word as seed, and we plant it all over the earth, until "in all the world . . . it is constantly bearing fruit and increasing" (Colossians 1:6).

It's always harvest time in one part of the world or another. In such a huge, all-encompassing vineyard, there is always a dire need of laborers. Jesus says to His disciples, " 'The harvest is plentiful, but the workers are few. Therefore beseech the Lord of the harvest to send out workers into His harvest' " (Matthew 9:37, 38; see also Luke 10:2). We've seen already that some are called to sow and some to water. Others are called to harvest. Jesus also points out that some are called to harvest that for which they have not labored. " 'Others have labored, and you have entered into their labor' " (John 4:38). We need to pay attention daily to what we are called to do, because it's usually a disaster if a reaper tries to sow, or vice versa. On the other hand, many times we are called to do all three at different times. We need to pay attention daily!

In order to have a good harvest, rain is necessary. According to the Bible, the rain that God's "crops" need is the Holy Spirit, and He has been pouring Himself out to a greater or lesser degree since He first hovered over the water at Creation. But since sin came into the world, shortly after that first hovering, heaven has been preparing for one great, world-wide harvest from this doomed planet. The patriarchs planted, the prophets watered and cultivated, and then the Son of God came to be planted and to die, and thus to fertilize the whole world with His blood. Not long after, the early rains came. In the Middle East, the early rains come in the fall and begin the flush of growth. In other climates, they come in the spring. There was a major early harvest after those early rains. Thousands accepted Jesus, and the new growth covered the known world in a generation. Since that time, down through the centuries, more planting, more watering, more cultivating, and ongoing harvests have been taking place. Soon, the Great Harvest will come, but before that time there will be a special outpouring of the Spirit called the latter rain.

> Rejoice, O sons of Zion, and be glad in the Lord your God; for He has given you the early rain for your vindication. And He has poured down for you the rain, the early and latter rain as before.... "And it will come about after this that I will pour out My Spirit on all mankind; and your sons and daughters will prophesy, your old men will dream dreams, your young men will see visions. And even on the male and female servants I will pour out My Spirit in those days. And I will display wonders in the sky and on the earth, blood, fire, and columns of smoke. The sun will be turned into darkness, and the moon into blood, before the great and awesome day of the Lord comes. And it will come about that whoever calls on the name of the Lord will be delivered" (Joel 2:23, 28-32).

It sounds awesome and exciting, but it also sounds scary, doesn't it? Jesus said those days would be so terrible that He would have to cut them short to save even the elect, His children! (See Matthew 24:20-24.) Believers might be imprisoned or hiding in the hills, and if they haven't learned to cling to God, if they haven't learned to bloom where they're planted, and not to base their happiness on outside circumstances, they'll be in serious trouble! But God has a goal we can't even imagine! Listen: " 'The exile will soon be set free, and will not die in the dungeon, nor will his bread be lacking. For I am the Lord your God, who stirs up the sea and its waves roar (the Lord of hosts is His name). And I have put My words in your mouth, and have covered you with the shadow of My hand, *to establish [plant] the heavens,* to found the earth, and to say to Zion, "You are My people" ' " (Isaiah 51:14-16, italics supplied.)

God wants to plant the heavens with you and me! He wants us to be able to tell the whole universe how He has triumphed over all odds.

And it all began because Jesus was willing to be planted in our dirty, diseased soil with and for us. Facing the end of His life on earth, He said, " 'Truly, truly, I say to you, unless a grain of wheat falls into the earth and dies, it remains by itself alone; but if it dies, it bears much fruit' " (John 12:24). I like to imagine that when the angel comforted Him in the Garden of Gethsemane, he might have reminded Jesus of what surely must have been one of His favorite texts: "As a result of the anguish of His soul, He will see it and be satisfied" (Isaiah 53:11).

That dark night, Jesus wasn't certain that He would prevail. He went ahead on faith—a faith that He had cultivated and developed His whole life, a faith that gave His heart comfort in that dark garden. And He won! He took firstfruits with Him to heaven when He went (see Matthew 27:51-53; Ephesians 4:8), and one of these days, you'll see Him reaping, and then standing on the sea of glass surrounded by His beloved harvest. And the glow in His eyes will leave no doubt that He is satisfied!

After all, He has *you*, doesn't He?

DIG DEEPER

The first paragraph of this chapter listed several "mini gardens." Are you like one of them—or something else? What kind of garden do you think God wants you to be right now? Write about it, and about how you can bloom your best right where you are planted.

List someone you know who fits into each of the categories in the parable of the sower. Plan your prayers to reflect what you know about their lives and attitudes, and ask God if there is anything else He wants you to do for that person besides pray faithfully.

Which category in the parable is most likely to tempt you? What will you do to combat it?

Has God planted you in security? Is it physical and temporal security—or spiritual security? Or both? How did He bring you where you are now? Have you thanked Him lately? Are you blooming where you are planted, even if it's not where you hope to be for long?

Do you know if you are called to be a planter, a waterer, or a reaper? If not, ask! How are you doing the work God has given you? Ask Him if there is anything He would like to change.

Are you praying for the latter rain of the Holy Spirit? Are you practicing now to cling to Him in trials so that when the promised trials come to the whole earth, you will be adept at holding on to something invisible and singing in the dark?

Originally, I planned to end this book with a "walk" through God's planted heavens—the Promised Land to which He will take all of us one day. I decided it was beyond my capability! Spend some time imagining (even writing about it, if you are braver than I am!), what you think it will be like to live and move and have your being in the visible hands of a *visible, touchable,* beloved Master Gardener! What a life that will be!

But that's tomorrow. Today it's still winter, still January. Everything is still cold and silent. Nothing seems to be alive. It's hard to believe tomorrow's harvest will ever come. But look through the warm, lighted windows of God's potting shed. There He is, doing the same thing He always does in the winter. He's poring over His seed catalogs and graph paper, eyes alight with anticipation. He's dreaming about you. Listen! Hear Him whispering your name? "And _____ will be like a tree firmly planted by streams of water, which yields its fruit in its season, and its leaf does not wither; and in whatever [s]he does, [s]he prospers" (Psalm 1:3).

If you enjoyed this book, you'll enjoy these as well:

Devotional Retreats
Debbonnaire Kovacs. Draw closer to Jesus through devotional retreats—a method of using your five senses to study God's Word. Kovacs explains the purpose and joy of Christian meditation, and how it differs from the New Age counterfeit.
0-8163-1837-9. Paperback.
US$10.99, Can$16.99.

God Said, "I Promise"
Debbonnaire Kovacs. The Ten Commandments are more than a list of DON'Ts. Debbonnaire Kovacs shows us how to look at God's law in a whole new way—as promises of things the Lord is already doing in our hearts and lives! For personal or small group study. [Discussion questions included!]
0-8163-1779-8. US$8.99, Can$13.99.

The Cure for Soul Fatigue
Karl Haffner. With lots of laugh therapy along the way, and megadoses of wisdom, pastor Karl exposes the root causes of soul fatigue and prescribes the biblical cures to remedy them. Learn how to win over worry. Banish the blues. Get your priorities in order. Deal with discouragement. Find forgiveness. Follow your life calling, and more.
0-8163-1840-9. US$10.99, Cdn$16.99.

Order from your ABC by calling **1-800-765-6955**, or get online and shop our virtual store at **www.adventistbookcenter.com**.

- Read a chapter from your favorite book
- Order online
- Sign up for email notices on new products

Prices subject to change without notice.